Paul's Gospel, Empire, Race, and Ethnicity

Paul's Gospel, Empire, Race, and Ethnicity

Through the Lens of Minoritized Scholarship

EDITED BY

Yung Suk Kim

PICKWICK *Publications* · Eugene, Oregon

PAUL'S GOSPEL, EMPIRE, RACE, AND ETHNICITY
Through the Lens of Minoritized Scholarship

Pickwick Publications
An Imprint of Wipf and Stock Publishers
199 W. 8th Ave., Suite 3
Eugene, OR 97401

www.wipfandstock.com

PAPERBACK ISBN: 978-1-6667-3187-3
HARDCOVER ISBN: 978-1-6667-2487-5
EBOOK ISBN: 978-1-6667-2488-2

Cataloguing-in-Publication data:

Names: Kim, Yung Suk [editor.]

Title: Paul's Gospel, empire, race, and ethnicity : through the lens of minoritized scholarship / edited by Yung Suk Kim.

Description: Eugene, OR: Pickwick Publications, 2023 | Includes bibliographical references.

Identifiers: ISBN 978-1-6667-3187-3 (paperback) | ISBN 978-1-6667-2487-5 (hardcover) | ISBN 978-1-6667-2488-2 (ebook)

Subjects: LCSH: Bible.—Epistles of Paul—Criticism, interpretation, etc. | Paul, the Apostle, Saint. | Ethnicity in the Bible. | Racism—Religious aspects—Christianity. | Group identity—Religious aspects. | Rome in the Bible. | Religion and politics—Rome—History.

Classification: BS2506.3 K56 2023 (print) | BS2506.3 (ebook)

02/20/23

Contents

Part III: Paul, Empire, and Community

Contributors

Yung Suk Kim, editor and contributor, is Professor of New Testament and Early Christianity at Virginia Union University. He received a PhD from Vanderbilt University and an MDiv from McCormick Theological Seminary. He authored many books, including *Monotheism, Biblical Traditions, and Race Relations* (2022); *How to Read Paul: A Brief Introduction to His Theology, Writing, and World* (2021); *Christ's Body in Corinth: The Politics of a Metaphor* (2008); and *Toward Decentering the New Testament* (Cascade 2018, co-authored with Mitzi J. Smith). He edited *1-2 Corinthians: Texts @ Contexts* (2013) and *Reading Minjung Theology in the Twenty-First Century* (Pickwick 2013, co-edited with Jin-Ho Kim).

Efraín Agosto is Visiting Professor of Latinx Studies and Religion at Williams College. He has also served as Professor of New Testament at New York Theological Seminary (2011–2021), and Professor of New Testament at Hartford Seminary (1995–2011). A Puerto Rican New Yorker, Efrain has a BA from Columbia University (1977), MDiv from Gordon-Conwell Theological Seminary (1982) and PhD from Boston University (1996). His publications include *Servant Leadership: Jesus and Paul* (2005), *Preaching in the Interim: Transitional Leadership in the Latino/a Church* (2018), and *Latinxs, the Bible and Migration* (co-edited with Jacqueline Hidalgo, 2018).

Jeehei Park is Assistant Professor of New Testament at Seminary of the Southwest. She has a PhD from Fordham University and an MDiv from Harvard Divinity School. Her research and teaching interests include race/ethnicity in the Roman world, material culture in early Christianity, and decolonial and postcolonial theories and theologies. Park's work has been recognized with several awards and fellowships including the Forum for Theological Exploration dissertation fellowship and the Louisville Institute postdoctoral fellowship. She is the author of *All Citizens of Christ: A Cosmopolitan Reading of Unity and Diversity in Paul's Letters* (2022).

Ekaputra Tupamahu is Assistant Professor of New Testament at Portland Seminary and George Fox University. He received his PhD from Vanderbilt University in 2019. He earned a master's degree and an MDiv from Asia Pacific Theological Seminary, and master's degrees from the Claremont School of Theology and Vanderbilt University. Tupamahu has a broad range of academic interests, including the politics of language, race/ethnic theory, postcolonial studies, immigration studies, critical study of religion, and global Christianity. He is the author of *Contesting Languages: Heteroglossia and the Politics of Language in the Early Church* (2022).

Sze-kar Wan is Professor of New Testament at Perkins School of Theology, Southern Methodist University. He received a ThD from Harvard University Divinity School and an MDiv from Gordon-Conwell Theological Seminary. Wan is the author of, *inter alia, Romans: Empire and Resistance; Power in Weakness: Conflict and Rhetorics in Paul's Second Letter to the Corinthians;* and co-editor of *Diverse Strands of a Common Thread: An Introduction to Ethnic Chinese Biblical Interpretation;* and *The Bible in Modern China: The Literary and Intellectual Impact.* His interests include Pauline studies, postcolonialism, Asian American hermeneutics, and Chinese Neo-Confucianism.

Demetrius K. Williams is an Associate Professor in the Department of Global Studies at UW-Milwaukee where he teaches in the Comparative Literature program. He received a ThD from Harvard University Divinity School and an MDiv also from Harvard. He is also an affiliated faculty member for the Religious Studies program. His most recent work is entitled, *The Cross of Christ in African American Christian Religious Experience: Piety, Politics, and Protest* (2023 forthcoming). His other publications include *"An End to This Strife": The Politics of Gender in African American Churches* (2004) and *"Enemies of the Cross of Christ": The Terminology of the Cross and Conflict in Philippians* (2002).

1

Introduction

Yung Suk Kim

I CONCEIVED A NEW book project when the tweets were going around social media right after the Atlanta Spa Shootings in which eight people were killed by a white man in March 2021, including six women of Asian descent. The senseless attacks sparked a furor and concern, particularly among Asian Americans, and compelled them to ask questions about race/ethnicity, identity, and belonging. See below the eclectic tweets prevalent at the time, which reveal an entangled mix of agony, struggle, confusion, and despair.

> The American concept of "Asian massage parlors" is rooted in anti-Asian racism, built on [the] idea that Asian women are exotic, submissive, and interchangeable.[1]

> NYPD says a 65-year-old Asian American woman was walking to church this morning when [a] suspect assaulted her and said "f*** you, you don't belong here."[2]

> My 5-year-old boy came home and asked me why [the] bigger kid kept calling him Chinese Boy. My son, confused, told the boy I'm a New Jersey Boy. He laughed it off, but my eyes welled up. 50

1. CATW International. Twitter post, March 29, 2021, 11:21 p.m. https://twitter.com/CATWIntl/status/1376736277224116224.

2. CeFaan Kim. Twitter post, March 29, 2021, 8:52 p.m. https://twitter.com/CeFaanKim/status/1376698713582796804.

years ago, my parents immigrated here but we cannot shake [the] shadow of foreignness.[3]

Ohio official and US Army vet Lee Wong on CNN: "It was just too much to bear that people came to me and told me that I don't look American enough or patriotic. I'm just as American as an apple pie. And I served this country honorably. And to say that to me, to my face, it hurts."[4]

Racism has been ingrained in the life of America since European settlement and colonialism. American Indians were treated as nobodies and expelled from their homes and lands. Hardly can we describe the magnitude and depth of the excruciating pain and trauma that African Americans have undergone for several hundred years, and the agony of racism never goes away easily. Refugees and immigrants came from all over the world—predominantly from Latin America—to pursue their dreams but faced xenophobia, racism, sexism, classism, and cultural imperialism.

With the overriding concerns about American life, I set my mind on gathering crucial voices from minoritized scholars who deal with the intersection between Paul's gospel, empire, and race/ethnicity. Contributors to this volume represent diverse cultures and perspectives of Asian descent, African American heritage, and Latin American culture. This collective volume is the clarion call that biblical interpretation is not an arcane genre in the ivory tower but engages current issues in the real world of America, where we must tackle racism, the Western imperial gospel, and the rigid body politic.

This book is divided into three parts: Part I. Paul, Gospel, and Empire; Part II. Paul, Empire, and Race/Ethnicity; and Part III. Paul, Empire, and Community. In Part I, two articles tackle Paul and his gospel in an imperial context. Yung Suk Kim, in his article, "The Politics of Interpretation: Paul's Gospel, Empire, and Race/Ethnicity," opens the door for the volume by setting its tone and theme around the politics of interpretation in Paul's letters. He revisits familiar topics such as the gospel, community, and body politics, and challenges the Western gospel that is focused on doctrine and the rhetoric of unity. His interpretation takes the faithfulness

---

3. Andy Kim. Twitter post, March 27, 2021, 10:23 a.m. https://twitter.com/AndyKimNJ/status/1375815775408259084.

4. Kyle Griffin. Twitter post, April 1, 2021, 12:30 p.m. https://twitter.com/kylegriffin1/status/1377659523935047680.

of Jesus seriously, which is the foundation for Paul's assemblies that embrace differences and diversity.

The second article in Part I comes from Efraín Agosto: "Paul the Apostle of the Nations and Pedro Albizu Campos, the Apostle of Puerto Rican Independence: A Comparative Study of Race, Ethnicity, and Empire." Agosto reads Paul with Pedro Albizu Campos (1891–1965), who is called the "Apostle of Puerto Rican Liberation." His comparative, contextual interpretation of Paul is interesting and incisive. He contrasts Paul with Albizu. While the former advocates for the marginalized in the Roman Empire and expected the Parousia in the near future, the latter focuses more on the radical, immediate liberation of Puerto Rico from the American empire. Agosto asks readers to rethink the role of the apostle and engage with Paul and his letters from their world of politics, economics, and culture. Accordingly, he conceives a broadly defined apostleship, which must elevate freedom, human dignity, and ethnic identity in the world.

In Part II, two articles focus on intersections between Paul, empire, and race/ethnicity. In "'Let This Mind Be in You': Paul and the Politics of Identity in Philippians—Empire, Ethnicity, and Justice," Demetrius K. Williams critiques white Evangelicalism that falsely subsumes race/ethnicity under the notion of triumphant identity in Christ and seeks to explore the "in-Christ identity" in the dramatic narratives of Christ in Phil 2:6–11 and Paul in 3:5–11. In the American historical context, Protestant missionaries and preachers used the Christ hymn in Phil 2:6–11 to nurture a Christology of suffering, inculcating their ideology of God in the enslaved population. Williams places the identity of Philippians in Christ Jesus who radically reimagined the world, based on love, justice, and solidarity. As they are exhorted to live with a distinct set of religious values from the empire, their identity in Christ does not mean they negate their culture or race/ethnicity. Williams argues that the African American church's quest for social justice is consistent with their ethnic identity in Christ.

The other article in Part II is "Mainstreaming the Minoritized: Galatians 3.28 as Ethnic Construction." In this article, Sze-kar Wan reads Paul as the apocalyptic Christian Jew who argues gentiles in Christ will be incorporated into "Eschatological Israel" eventually. Before that happens, gentile Christians are not required to become Jewish. Wan eloquently and skillfully challenges the long-held Western interpretation/ideology of Christian unity/race/identity at the expense of Jews and all other cultures. At the same time, Wan cautions against the popular reading of Gal 3:28

3

that comes with a radical social justice orientation. Paul is certainly Jewish ethnocentric, thinking from a Jewish perspective, but he overcomes his ethnocentrism to include gentiles as the descendants of Abraham through faith. Ethnicities or differences are not denied in the Christian community; they can maintain their own cultural heritage while staying in Christ. In the end, Wan's reading helps readers see the limitations of Gal 3:28 because it does not directly deal with an unequal society. He also adds the fact that Paul is not a universalist who forges the new humanity in Christ apart from ethnicities or cultures.

In Part III, two articles focus on intersections between Paul, empire, and community, and the contributors read Galatians and Romans from Diaspora perspectives. Jeehei Park, in her article, "The Pursuit of Impossible Hospitality: Reading Paul's *Philoxenia* with Jacques Derrida," reexamines *philoxenia* in Rom 12:13b—a Pauline *hapax legomenon* that is usually translated as "hospitality." Unsettling familiar notions of hospitality in the empire through Derrida's concept of radical impossible hospitality, Park explores Paul's hospitality as an impossible yet possible act of radicalism that goes beyond any empire, culture, and tradition. She reads Romans from a foreigner's perspective and disrupts an imperial order that perpetuates the dominant culture's hegemony in society. She seeks to explore "home" in the land of a white-centric empire. Park's ultimate question is about the politics of power and identity in which the central question is who has the power to offer such hospitality and whether the host's hospitality is radical enough to blur divisive boundaries and embrace others as they are.

The last essay in Part III is "From Alienation to Inclusion: Reading Romans 3:21–26 from a Diaspora Lens." In this article, Ekaputra Tupamahu reads the passage from a diaspora perspective—from his diaspora experience in America. Against the doctrinal reading of atonement in this passage, Tupamahu investigates Paul's diaspora experience and reinterprets the passage. He argues that Rom 3:21–26 is not about an abstract teaching of salvation or individual justification. But it reflects Paul's struggle and his experience of alienation and exclusion in the Roman world where he pursues "true belonging" to God through Christ. Tupamahu's diaspora reading of Rom 3:21–26 challenges the normative, doctrinal reading that does not delve into Paul's diaspora experience in the real world where he struggles to understand his place and identity.

In closing, I wish to express my deepest thanks to all my contributors. On the one hand, they make effort to unravel and unsettle the contents and strategies of the Western gospel, the hegemonic community, and the white-centered, monolithic culture. On the other, they explore the implications and ramifications of Paul's gospel for race/ethnicity in America as well as in the Roman Empire. Never do they portray Paul as the perfect apostle but take him seriously in context by refocusing on his gospel and view of empire and race/ethnicity. While Paul is not a political revolutionary or social reformer, his gospel is not simply otherworldly or dualistic in that he denies participation in this world. Rather, the empire is denounced and relegated by his rhetorical strategy that God is the ultimate source of good news. The harbinger of the gospel is not an emperor but Jesus, the Son of God, who manifested God's righteousness to the world. Jesus is the foundation of the *ekklesia* whose members must follow him, edifying the community with mutual respect and solidarity, affirming the diverse gifts of the Spirit, and acknowledging all differences. In the end, biblical interpretation is not apolitical. Which Paul do we read? While we must take a stand, we must be wary of hegemonic interpreters who do not see the complexity and diversity of Paul's thoughts and his world.

PART I

Paul, Gospel, and Empire

2

The Politics of Interpretation

Paul's Gospel, Empire, and Race/Ethnicity

YUNG SUK KIM

DIFFERENT PEOPLE INTERPRET PAUL differently and adopt him for their argument. Whoever reads his letters, their reading must be contextual because the reader presupposes an ideal world, community, and society in their interpretation. Interpreters always make choices about their context, reading lens, and textual methods,[1] and they cannot avoid the embeddedness of politics in their interpretation—which leads to the politics of interpretation. Often different interpreters vie for their position, but not all of their interpretations are equally useful or valid. So, it is important to expose their interpretations of Paul to testing, as Paul himself says: "Test everything and hold fast to what is good" (1 Thess 5:21). In this chapter, we will examine Paul's gospel and its relationship to empire and race/ethnicity, testing the interpretations of others, and exploring the intersection among them.[2]

---

1. Kim, *Biblical Interpretation*, 1–44.

2. I have explored Paul's gospel in numerous publications. See Kim, *Rereading Romans from the Perspective of Paul's Gospel; Rereading Galatians from the Perspective of Paul's Gospel; Christ's Body in Corinth; Reimagining the Body of Christ in Paul's Letters; A Theological Introduction to Paul's Letters.*

Paul and the Western Gospel

In Western Christianity, Paul is considered a champion of the good news or the gospel (*euangelion*) characterized by "justification by faith." His primary, theological concern is understood as how an individual is justified once and for all—usually from a forensic salvation perspective. That is, one needs only *faith in Christ*, which means accepting his salvific, redemptive death. So, the *pistis christou* phrases in Rom 3:22–26 and Gal 2:16–21 are translated as "faith in Christ" (the objective genitive), and there is no emphasis on "the faithfulness of Christ" (the subjective genitive).[3] Likewise, believers of this gospel are taught that the church as "the body of Christ" (1 Cor 12:27; Rom 12:4–5) is a unified community in Christ that subsumes all other cultures and differences. In this traditional body politics, the emphasis is on doctrine and membership. Community members are one because they belong to the community of Christ. Otherwise, there is not enough room for engaging in diversity and differences in the community.

The Western gospel goes back to the Reformation where the central doctrine is "justification by faith" apart from works. Faith is objectified as knowledge or teaching, and the Western churches and missionaries were convinced that they had the truth of the gospel.[4] During Western colonialism in the nineteenth century, they went to less developed countries with commercial ships and propagated the gospel of prosperity, rejecting indigenous cultures, and devaluing the "primitive" lifestyles of local people.[5] In a way, the Western gospel spread along with colonialism and commerce. Modernized schools and hospitals were established to educate local people and cure the sick. But this gospel did not touch on politics or teach people how to fight evil or injustices in society. For example, Protestant missionaries in Korea in the nineteenth century were silent about the Japanese invasion and its brutal rule. Instead, they chose not to be involved in politics.

---

3. Elsewhere in my publications, I have argued for the subjective genitive reading of πίστις Χριστοῦ in Rom 3:21–26, Gal 2:16–21, Phil 3:9 (all these references from Paul's authentic letters). That is, Paul emphasizes "Christ's faithfulness" through which God's righteousness has been manifested to the world (Rom 3:21–22). If he meant an objective genitive, i.e., "faith in Christ," he could have used a prepositional phrase, *pistis en christo*, for example, τὴν πίστιν ὑμῶν ἐν Χριστῷ Ἰησοῦ as in Col 1:4. The similar phrases are in the Deutero-Pauline and Pastoral letters: 1 Tim 1:4; 3:13; 2 Tim 1:13; 3:15. See Kim, *How to Read Paul*, 75–89; Kim, *Theological Introduction to Paul's Letters*, 63–82.

4. Underwood, *Call of Korea*. See also Kim, "Reevaluating Western Mission and Mission Texts."

5. Hutchison, *Errand to the World*.

Strictly speaking, they participated in politics by not involving themselves directly in the world. In a way, their silence is also a form of political action because they helped the status quo of society.

Long before Luther, Augustine romanticized or spiritualized the Christian gospel as a matter of "inner heart" that the essence of Christianity is "faith which is believed" (*fides quae creditur*) and "faith by which it is believed" (*fides qua creditur*).[6] In the former, faith is identical to knowledge, and in the latter, faith is like conviction by which one can believe unbelievable things. Otherwise, participatory faith in Christ or Christ's faithfulness to God's righteousness is not in view. For Augustine, faith is confined to matters of the heart, and salvation is understood in a legal concept that one is declared innocent by a judge. Luther inherited Augustine's theology and cemented the doctrine of justification by faith at the expense of anti-semitism, which is the result of his separation between faith and the law.[7]

The Western gospel comes with the ideology of unity that no other truths or different understandings of the gospel are allowed. All members of the church or society must think in the same way. Likewise, Western interpreters and their followers have read "the body of Christ" in 1 Cor 12:12–27 and Rom 12:4–5 as an organism metaphor, emphasizing membership in Christ and doctrine. Members are supposed to teach and follow the same doctrine and accept the higher governing bodies. This Western gospel is operative with the attitude of "we have or know the truth." Here, "we" refers to "white" readers, who think they have salvific knowledge and that others must follow their teaching, which is "justification by faith." It is a w(hit)e-centered gospel. Some white Christians think that their race, culture, and civilization are superior to others.[8] To maintain their supremacy, they marketize this gospel as a commodity that attracts other people and guarantees prosperity and stability for them. To sell this product, the Western gospel promoters established schools and dominated academic disciplines. On the other hand, this gospel is easily translated into pride and arrogance, allowing believers to conquer other religions and cultures. In this atmosphere, anti-Judaism and relegation of other cultures are prevalent among them.

6. This view of faith is found in the Deutero-Pauline and Pastoral Letters. After Paul died, churches became conservative and adopted the social convention of hierarchy and gender division. See Kim, *How to Read Paul*, 27–35. See also Kim, *Theological Introduction to Paul's Letters*, 79–80. See also Wan, "Mainstreaming the Minoritized."

7. Luther, "Jews and Their Lies."

8. NPR, "White Supremacist Ideas Have Historical Roots In U.S. Christianity."

The above atmosphere in the Western gospel is conducive to conquering other religions. In Korea, some Christians entered Buddhist temples and destroyed their sacred items to cleanse the land. Some Korean churches sent youth and young adults as short-term missionaries to less developed countries in Southeast Asia. Some of these young people entered Mosques and Buddhist shrines and prayed a Christian prayer and sang hymns, thinking that they might conquer them with the power of the gospel. Many Korean churches and Christians bought this Western gospel and are now exporting it to other countries. They think they have the truth of the gospel, favoring the Western lifestyle, prosperity, and power. They go everywhere to sell this specific knowledge-based "gospel" and tell people that they are justified once and for all. Otherwise, justification is never understood in a moral or ethical sense that they must participate in Christ or in God's justice. Ethics is secondary to salvation, and social justice never becomes essential or intrinsic to the gospel. This Western gospel goes well with individualism and capitalism. People feel good about themselves and seek power and prosperity as a sign of God's blessing. While some emphasize participatory faith in Christ, they do not consider Jesus's faithfulness, maintaining a dichotomy between faith and the law or works.

Paul and the Truth of the Gospel

Paul proclaimed the gospel to the gentiles and his gospel is rooted in God. He begins Rom 1:1, saying he is called an apostle and set apart for "the gospel of God" (εὐαγγέλιον Θεοῦ, Rom 1:1). God is the one who promised the good news "beforehand through his prophets in the holy scriptures" (Rom 1:2). Jesus is the one who proclaimed the good news of God and demonstrated God's righteousness to the world. He "was descended from David according to the flesh and was declared to be Son of God with power according to the spirit of holiness by resurrection from the dead, Jesus Christ our Lord" (Rom 1:4). Jesus's faithfulness and his work of God constitutes the gospel of Christ, which is understood in two ways: the good news that Jesus proclaimed; the good news about him because of his grace. Christians "have received grace and apostleship to bring about the obedience of faith among all the gentiles for the sake of his name" (Rom 1:5).

As we see above, Paul's gospel comes with a threefold formula: "the gospel of God," "the gospel of Christ," and "the gospel that Christians proclaim through Christ."[9] The gospel of God means God is the beginning of the good news. God called Abraham out of nowhere and made a covenant with him because he trusted God. God's covenantal love extended to the gentiles through the same faith, as Rom 3:30 confirms this point: "Since God is one; and he will justify the circumcised on the ground of faith and the uncircumcised through that same faith." God's good news has been proclaimed and manifested to the world through Christ's faithfulness (Rom 3:22a). That is, God's love and justice have been revealed through Christ's work and his faithfulness. But that is not the end of the story because the followers of Christ must have "the faithfulness of Jesus" (Rom 3:26).

The Truth of the Gospel in Galatians

Paul explores the truth of the gospel in Galatians against those who argue that gentiles need Jewish laws in addition to faith and that they should be circumcised. He presents his own scriptural argument that is based on Abraham's call story and God's grace (Gen 12). His point is that by God's grace and his initiative, Abraham embarked on a new journey of faith. Before the law was given, Abraham trusted God and walked by faith. So, Paul argues faith comes before the law. Faith makes a new journey possible through the grace of God. But Paul's opponents (Jewish Christians) argue differently, based on Gen 17 where Abraham and his descendants are instructed to be circumcised without conditions because they are covenant people. According to Gen 17, circumcision is not negotiable and is a condition for staying in a covenantal community. So, they are not wrong because their interpretation is also rooted in the text.

The politics of interpretation occurs between Paul and his counterparts. On the one hand, Paul acknowledges two versions of the gospel, as he says in Gal 2:7: "On the contrary, when they saw that I had been entrusted with the gospel for the uncircumcised, just as Peter had been entrusted with the gospel for the circumcised." Jewish customs and laws are perfectly applicable to Jews while they stay in Christ's faithfulness. But those things should not be imposed on the gentiles because the essential thing for them is "faith working through love" (Gal 5:6). Paul believes love fulfills the law: "For the whole law is summed up in a single commandment, 'You shall love your neighbor as yourself'" (Gal 5:14). Ultimately, however, Paul does

9. Kim, *How to Read Paul*, 49–62; *Rereading Romans from the Perspective of Paul's Gospel*, 4–15; Kim, "Which Gospel Do We Preach?"

not say that there are two different gospels; rather, the gospel is one and the same for all, Jews and gentiles alike. That is, all people need to come to faith through *Christ and faith*.[10] The law can be discerned and kept with a focus on the love of God and the love of neighbor.

The Truth of the Gospel in Romans

Paul writes a letter to the Roman Christians mainly for three reasons. First, he tells gentile Christians that his gospel ("the gospel that he proclaims") is not law-free but law-affirming in ways that they must love their neighbors (Rom 13:8–10). Many gentile Christians misunderstood Paul's gospel, thinking that faith alone is enough. But Paul says that faith cannot overthrow the law (Rom 3:31), and the latter is fulfilled through the former. Moreover, following the way of Christ, which means participating in his faith, fulfills the law (Rom 10:4). Likewise, Paul also tells the gentile Christians that they should not judge Israel or the Jews because God is still loving and faithful toward Israel (Rom 11:26–36). Second, Paul tells Jewish Christians that his gospel is not anti-Jewish or against the law. Many Jewish Christians thought that Paul was against Israel or the law. But he says the law is holy and its commandments are good and perfect (Rom 7:12). But he also tells them that their priority is not the law or law absolutism but *faith and Christ* together. Here the concept of the common gospel for all applies, as we saw before. There is no separate gospel for the Jews. They also need faith and Christ, and the only difference is they may keep Jewish traditions and laws for their faithful religious life as long as they have faith and follow Jesus. Third, Paul writes this letter to garner support from the Roman Christians when he goes on to the Spanish mission. He needs financial and spiritual support from them to accomplish his dream to proclaim the gospel of God to the end of the earth, which is Spain. Before going to Rome, he needs to share his faith that does not reject the law or Israel, clearing some misunderstandings about his gospel.

In sum, Romans is about the gospel of God, which is none other than "the power of God for salvation to everyone who has faith, to the Jew first and also to the Greek" (Rom 1:16). Paul is eager to spread this good news of God that was proclaimed and confirmed by Jesus, who showed faithfulness

---

10. Kim, "Which Gospel Do We Preach?" Paul points out the importance of both Christ and faith. It is Christ who fulfilled the promise of God through faith. Therefore, Christians must also live by the faithfulness of Jesus.

to God and revealed God's righteousness. All who follow Jesus must live like him, dying with him, and being led by the Spirit. Jesus's death alone is not enough; those who follow him must die with him, which means "by the Spirit to put to death the deeds of the body" (Rom 8:13). Furthermore, "For all who are led by the Spirit of God are children of God" (Rom 8:14).

Paul's Gospel and Empire

Paul's gospel is not overtly political although it sounds political and has political implications for his Christian assemblies. For example, Rom 13:1–10 sounds political but his tone is defensive rather than challenging the empire. He cautions against Christians' disobedience to the higher governing bodies and asks them to cooperate with them by paying taxes. But carefully interpreted in context, this text does not seem to suggest condoning evil or injustices in society by giving blind obedience to the authorities. Rather, Paul is concerned about giving the wrong impression/message to the authorities that Christians are anti-social or anti-imperial. In such a situation, his assemblies could not survive or the empire would not tolerate them. This conservative position by Paul is due to his apocalyptic thinking that the Lord would come back soon when God will intervene in the world to make corrections, including social and political structures. With this interim ethics, Paul's message has political implications and morally high standards. For example, in 1 Cor 7:17–24, his basic stance is, "Do your best in your place and show the world that you reflect the light of God to the world." He says Christians were bought with a price and therefore, they should not become "slaves of humans" (1 Cor 7:23). Certainly, this statement does not seem logical because some Corinthians are indeed slaves of humans. Most likely what Paul means is metaphorical in that they must give their loyalty to God, not to humans. Likewise, he uses slavery as a metaphor throughout his letters. That is unsavory to many who take slavery seriously and as morally wrong. In 1 Cor 7:24, Paul summarizes his apocalyptic, conservative view of the world: "In whatever condition you were called, brothers and sisters, there remain with God." But we should not forget that apocalyptic thinking is also radical in the sense that the empire's permanent establishment with the propaganda of "peace and security" will collapse eventually because of God's intervention. The issue is a matter of time. So, we can also say that Paul is conservative because he did not directly intervene in the world to change the system although he emphasizes Christian moral duty. His moral standards are very high, comparable to Jesus's teaching in the Sermon on the Mount (e.g., Matt 5:38–48) where he emphasizes no retaliation and unconditional love, including the love of the enemies. In Rom 12:21, he summarizes Christian moral responsibility toward others in society: "Do not be overcome by evil, but overcome evil with good."

The Body of Christ (σῶμα Χριστοῦ, *Soma Christou*), Empire, and Race/Ethnicity

In Stoicism, the body is used as a metaphor for a hierarchical organism. Stoic philosophers argue society is one and structured hierarchically. All members belong to the same society and are advised to stick to the norm of unity (*homonoia*). Otherwise, the Stoics do not care for the marginalized or advocate for them. Elites and rulers are at the center of society, and all others serve those at the top. In the body metaphor, many parts work together for one body, and their relationships with each other are hierarchical. Namely, the head is the command center, the belly is a storehouse, and the hands and legs are the workers. The ideology of hierarchical unity is told in the fable of Menenius Agrippa.[11] That is, working parts (hands and feet) should not rebel against the stomach even if the stomach eats food all the time without working like other parts. If the working parts strike against the stomach and do not work, not only the stomach is going to die but the whole body will collapse. By implication, the fable suggests that slaves must work hard and stay in their place without complaining or rebelling against society.

Many biblical scholars borrow this idea of unity from Stoicism and apply it to Paul's texts such as 1 Cor 12:12–27 and Rom 12:4–5.[12] The unity-centered, Western interpretation of the body of Christ in 1 Cor 12:12–27 has dominated New Testament scholarship. The biggest problem is what I term "w(hit)e-centered unity with spurious diversity." When people say the community or the church is one, they already know who or what is at the center. It is unified thinking or doctrine by which all are bound. If there is one center, all other parts must serve it. By implication, if Christ is the center, the leader/pastor of a community takes the next position after him. The tricky part is the leader/pastor claims that he/she represents Christ

11. Livy, *History of Rome* 2.32.8–12.

12. Mitchell, *Paul and the Rhetoric of Reconciliation*. See also Lee, *Paul, the Stoics, and the Body of Christ*.

and his teaching. In the worst-case scenario, the language of unity falls into the rhetoric of control and sameness. Along this line of unity, we see the rising number of white supremacists, hegemonic theologians, and like-minded imitators of the center. Their view of the center is white privilege, elitism, intellectualism, and individualism. Certain attitudes about life, ideologies, or particular experiences dominate the community, church, or society. They also talk about diversity, but this diversity is spurious and no differences are tolerated or allowed. The margin or periphery remains perpetual and is used to celebrate the center. Spurious diversity is no more than dry flowers or fake flowers on the table. With this notion of unity and diversity, what is emphasized is sameness, membership, belonging, and order. All members must have the same doctrine (with no room for discussion of other views), receive membership training to maintain the same doctrine, and know their place in a hierarchy. In this context, faith means absolute obedience to higher governing bodies: God, Jesus, and leaders of the church. With this view of the center, those ingroups feel superior to others and their cultures, becoming racist, sexist, and elitist.

The Body of Christ as the Christic body

I see the body of Christ in 1 Cor 12:27 as a metaphor for "a way of living."[13] "The body of Christ" may be understood differently with the use of the attributive genitive ("Christic body" or Christ-like body), as we see another example of the attributive genitive in Rom 6:6: "We know that our old self was crucified with him so that *the body of sin* (τὸ σῶμα τῆς ἁμαρτίας) might be destroyed, and we might no longer be enslaved to sin." Here, "the body of sin" can be translated as "the sinful body or sin-ruled body." Likewise, "the body of Christ" means "Christ-full or Christ-ruled body." With this understanding, 1 Cor 12:27a may be translated as "You (Corinthians) are the Christic body" and "individually members of it" in 12:27b may be paraphrased as "individually and communally." With all these combined, 1 Cor 12:27 (ὑμεῖς δέ ἐστε σῶμα Χριστοῦ καὶ μέλη ἐκ μέρους) has a new translation: "You (plural) are the Christic body, individually and communally." This translation implies that the Corinthians must embody Christ and follow his spirit and faithfulness. The body is used as a metaphor for a way of life,

---

13. Kim, *How to Read Paul*, 121–33; Kim, *Christ's Body in Corinth*, 65–95; Kim, *Theological Introduction to Paul's Letters*, 83–108; Kim, *Reimagining the Body of Christ in Paul's Letters*, 30–39; Kim, "Reclaiming Christ's Body (*soma christou*)," 20–29.

which is also seen in 1 Cor 6:14–20. That is, the Corinthians must be united to Christ because they constitute the body, which is Christ. Their union with him means they imitate his faithfulness. That is also the way to glorify God in their body. In 1 Cor 12:27, Paul does not say the church (*ekklesia*) is the body; rather, he says "You (the Corinthians) are the Christic body." In fact, whenever he refers to the church, he uses "the church of God" (1 Cor 1:2; 10:32; 11:32; 15:9; 2 Cor 1:1; Gal 1:13).[14] We must see the difference between Paul's authentic letters and later epistles such as in the Deutero-Pauline letters (Col 1:18, 24; Eph 5:23) where the body of Christ is equated with the church, whose head is Christ.[15] In Col 1:18, "He is the head of the body, the church; he is the beginning, the firstborn from the dead, so that he might come to have first place in everything" (cf, Col 2:9; Eph 4:12, 15).[16] However, in 1 Corinthians 12, "you" (ὑμεῖς, the Corinthians) constitute the community, which is egalitarian because this community is operative with the same dignity to all members and because there is no hierarchy established within different parts. Christ is never said to be the head of the body. All parts (members) of the community work together to embody Christ, and their relationships are interdependent.

Ekklesia, Empire, and Race/Ethnicity

The above alternative interpretation reconfigures *ekklesia* and its implications for race/ethnicity. The "body of Christ" makes *ekklesia* exist. First, the body of Christ is reimagined as Christ crucified, which appears as showing God's weakness and foolishness but reveals God's strength and wisdom (1 Cor 1:18–25). Jesus Christ is the foundation of the church, not the head or center (1 Cor 3:11). At the center of the foundation lies his faithfulness, grace, and love for God and the world. Second, when "the body of Christ" in 1 Cor 12:27 is reinterpreted as the Christic body, which embodies Christ individually and communally, *ekklesia* provides an alternative politics to the empire, which is non-violent, political change through higher ethical standards, as in Rom 12:14–21. Third, the *ekklesia* movement embracing the Christic embodiment can acknowledge and celebrate differences in race/ethnicity because Christ represents service, care, grace, and love for others. The message about the cross is paradoxical, as summarized in 1

14. Kim, *How to Read Paul*, 122.

15. Kim, *How to Read Paul*, 122.

16. Kim, *Theological Introduction to Paul's Letters*, 104.

Cor 1:25: "For God's foolishness is wiser than human wisdom, and God's weakness is stronger than human strength." Jesus affirmed God's radical love of the weak, foolish, and despised (1 Cor 1:26–28). From the perspective of the empire, lifting the powerless and uneducated is a foolish thing. But Jesus advocates for them; the result is his cross. But God's caring love and justice are shown on that cross (c.f., 1 Cor 1:26–29). Otherwise, the cross itself is not the gospel. Jesus faithfully demonstrates God's righteousness that takes care of the marginalized. Fourth and lastly, the *ekklesia* movement should be ethically united with Christ, which is the community where all parts—in all their distinct differences—work together in solidarity. This community is understood not as a competition or hierarchy but as a union of different parts. While this union entails uneasiness, patience, vulnerability, and empathy, true diversity and solidarity may be achieved through that union with Christ.

Conclusion

While the Western gospel with the unity-driven community idea is entrenched in many people's minds and scholarship alike, we must seek the truth of the gospel constantly. Paul's gospel is not a victorious, imperial gospel that rejects other cultures or religions. We should be mindful of whose gospel we proclaim. Do we proclaim the gospel of God that Jesus carried until he died? Do we understand Paul's gospel where he audaciously included gentiles as who they are? By way of summary, below I list characteristics of Paul's relationship with Judaism, his gospel, and theology.

First, he did not leave Judaism or reject the law because of Christ or faith. His main thinking is that God's covenant extended to the gentiles through Christ and that the law is fulfilled through *Christ and faith*. In other words, Paul emphasizes both Christ's work (that is, his faithfulness) and Christians' participation in him. God justifies those who have "the faithfulness of Jesus" (τὸν ἐκ πίστεως Ἰησοῦ, Rom 3:26).

Second, Paul's view of Jesus's death is not as a sin offering as in propitiation or expiation, but the result of his faithful work of God for demonstrating God's righteousness, as indicated in Rom 3:21–26, Gal 2:16–21, and 1 Cor 1:18–25. Namely, Jesus's testimony to God's love and justice led to his death. But God made him live though Jesus was crucified *by weakness* (2 Cor 13:4).[17]

17. *Ex astheneias* in 2 Cor 13:4 may be translated as "by or because of weakness" rather

Third, Paul's gospel is not primarily about an individual justification by faith but about the inclusion of the gentiles into the house of God, which was promised by God through Abraham (Gal 3:1–29). In Rom 15:16, Paul thinks he is the last-day apostle and priest who brings the gentiles into the house of God through the gospel of God that was exemplified by Jesus. For this task, he is "a minister of Christ Jesus to the gentiles in the priestly service of the gospel of God, so that the offering of the gentiles may be acceptable, sanctified by the Holy Spirit."

Fourth, faith is not knowledge or conviction about God or Jesus but accepting God's promise and following Christ through his grace. It does not abolish the law but perfects it, as Rom 3:31 indicates: "Do we then overthrow the law by this faith? By no means! On the contrary, we uphold the law." The problem is not the law per se but the use of it by some people who argue for its absolute condition.

Fifth, Paul's gospel is different from the Western gospel and involves threefold features of the gospel: "the gospel of God"; "the gospel of Christ"; "the gospel that Christians carry to embody God's righteousness."[18] The good news does not begin with Jesus but with God. That is, God is the beginning of the good news. Jesus carried out the good news of God and was killed because of that. But God's righteousness was demonstrated through Christ's work and his faithful life. All this is the gospel of Christ. Christians received the grace of God and Jesus; they continue to live out the good news of God and the good news of Christ. They are a letter of Christ (2 Cor 3:3).

Sixth, Paul's gospel is not a unity-driven, imperial gospel but a Christ-informed union embracing solidarity and diversity. While unity (*homonoia*) is the language of oneness and control, as it is used by the Roman Empire and today's empires as well, the idea of union gives us a different image of a Christian community that is united to Christ, following his faith and his spirit (1 Cor 6:12–20). Understood this way, Paul's gospel does not support the American melting pot where white culture or the Western gospel is at its center.

Seventh, Paul's stance on the Roman imperium is a bit complex and implicit in some respects. For sure, he is not a political revolutionary or

than "in weakness," which connotes the idea of vicarious, redemptive sacrifice. That is, Paul emphasizes Jesus's unwanted yet unavoidable death due to his work of God. In this verse, we see the parallels between Jesus's weakness and God's power: Jesus was crucified by weakness, but God made him live by his power. See Kim, *Messiah in Weakness*.

18. Kim, *Theological Introduction to Paul's Letters*. See also Kim, "'Imitators' (*Mimetai*) in 1 Cor. 4:16 and 11:1*,*" 147–70.

abolitionist. But that does not mean that he is a supporter of the empire because his theology is challenging, as seen in 1 Cor 1:18–25. Basically, his body politics is egalitarian, as in Gal 3:28 and elsewhere (1 Cor 18:25), and his theology is dangerous to the empire because he reverses the worldview of Stoicism in that the elites rule the world. In his alternative view of the world, he declares: "God's foolishness is wiser than human wisdom, and God's weakness is stronger than human strength" (1 Cor 1:25). So, Paul's lukewarm social position is due to his interim ethics that he believes Jesus the Lord would return soon to turn all things upside down. That is why he does not try to change the social system, but he works hard to change human minds through Christ.

Eighth, Paul's view of the slavery system is nuanced. On the one hand, he does not support it, unlike the authors responsible for household codes found in the Deutero-Pauline and Pastoral texts. But on the other hand, he does not intend to abolish it, maybe because of his view of interim ethics. So ultimately, his view of egalitarian ethics or liberation hermeneutics in Gal 3:28 is limited and not applicable to society. Rather, his point in Gal 3:28 is the inclusion of the gentiles into the household of God.

Ninth and lastly, Paul has a very positive view of women, who pray and prophesy at worship along with men and receive the Holy Spirit equally with men (1 Cor 11—14). Junia, the wife of Andronicus, was the foremost apostle according to Paul (Rom 16:7). Phoebe was a minister of the church in Cenchrea, and Priscilla was a co-worker with Paul. The authentic Paul should not be confused with the portrayal of him in the Deutero-Pauline and Pastoral Letters regarding women.

3

Paul the Apostle of the Nations and Pedro Albizu Campos, the Apostle of Puerto Rican Independence

A Comparative Study of Empire and Resistance

EFRAÍN AGOSTO

Introduction: Another Apostle

IN THE ENGLISH-SPEAKING WORLD of the United States, little is known about the twentieth-century Puerto Rican Independence Movement leader, Pedro Albizu Campos (1891–1965). Yet, he was often referred to as the "Apostle of Puerto Rican Independence" or "Apostle of Puerto Rican Liberation."[1] In this essay, I would like to put him in conversation with the better-known apostle of the Christian Testament, Paul of Tarsus. First, I will review some of the life and times of Albizu Campos, including some of the religious influences that drove him toward demanding the independence of Puerto Rico from the United States, which he identified as an imperial presence. Albizu was a devout Roman Catholic, who thought

---

1. For example, in 1953, one Buenos Aires, Argentina newspaper made reference to Albizu's "apostleship" shortly after his release from prison in Puerto Rico (only to be re-arrested a year later; see discussion below): "Linchamiento Atomico de un Martir de la Libertad" in *Verdad* (Buenos Aires, Argentina, 1953), February, 1:24–27, cited by Nelson Denis, *War Against All Puerto Ricans*, 235. According to Denis, the appellation, "apostle of Puerto Rican independence," with reference to Albizu Campos appeared during his travels to Latin America in the late 1920s.

22

that Spanish Catholicism had been re-constituted into a distinctive Caribbean ethos over the centuries, creating a "nationalist Catholicism" that was a source of identity and culture for Puerto Rico as well as other Caribbean islands and Latin America. Albizu's lecture tours of other Latin American nations in the late 1920s as a powerful spokesperson for Puerto Rican independence also sought to align Puerto Rico with Latin America instead of North America. It was on these trips that the notion of an "apostleship" was first noted and it stuck.

In brief, Albizu's vision included an "Iberian-American" identity for Puerto Rico, which he believed would disappear over time under US auspices.[2] Thus, his advocacy included strong identity with the Island's Spanish history, fraught as it was given four hundred years of Spanish colonization (1492–1898). These ties to Spanish legacy included his strong Roman Catholic piety, as demonstrated by historian Anthony Stevens-Arroyo.[3] After his "apostolic" travels throughout Latin America in the late 1920s, Albizu's essays and speeches during the 1930s galvanized the island's efforts toward independence. However, the movement he led was stopped in its tracks by pushback from the US-appointed government and police forces on the Island, including violence against organized independence protests. By 1937, Albizu and several key nationalist leaders were arrested and convicted of sedition and sent off to federal prison in Atlanta.

Albizu did not return to the Island until 1947 but by then the forces for an intermediary status for Puerto Rico, the Commonwealth status, were strong, led by the popular first-elected governor of Puerto Rico (1948), Luis Muñoz Marin. Albizu spoke eloquently, forcefully, and determinedly for three years against this move, ultimately deciding with other members and participants in the Nationalist Party that an outright revolt would bring attention to the cause of independence more than anything else. The efforts, which turned violent, failed, and Albizu was once again arrested and sent to jail, for most of the rest of his life (1950–1965, except for a short-lived

2. Pedro Albizu Campos's father was Alejandro Albizu Romero, the son of a well-to-do Basque family in Ponce, Puerto Rico. His mother, Julia Campos, a servant in that family household, was a Black woman, whose parents had been slaves. She died while Pedro was still a child, and an aunt raised him. As is the custom in Latin America, including in Puerto Rico, one carries both the father's and mother's names. We will alternate in this essay between using both names or just his father's. Alejandro Albizu did not recognize Pedro as his son until the latter was already a student at Harvard University in the late 1910s.

3. Stevens-Arroyo, "Catholic Worldview in the Political Philosophy of Pedro Albizu Campos," 53–73.

release in 1953–1954). Thereafter, cries for independence lost ground in Puerto Rico, and, in fact, statehood has gained greater force, although not enough, given the economic hardships on the Island, especially recently. Many in the US Congress, which has ultimate power over what happens in Puerto Rico, shy away from supporting statehood for this still culturally distinct Caribbean Island. Thus, the status as a "Freely Associated State," the Puerto Rican constitutional name, in Spanish, for the English term "Commonwealth," which Muñoz Marin argued would be temporary, remains. Albizu was right, in the estimation of many today, including this author, freedom would be illusive unless it was complete.[4]

Connections between Pedro and Paul? Empire

Readers of this volume might ask of this Pauline New Testament scholar, "What does Pedro Albizu Campos have to do with Apostle Paul?" We turn, then, toward several themes in this essay in a proposed dialogue between Pedro and Paul. First, there is the question of *empire*.

Albizu Campos and the US Empire

Pedro Albizu Campos was clear in his denunciation of what he saw as the imperial presence and practices of the US in Puerto Rico since its invasion in 1898. Albizu understood what had happened to Puerto Rico at the turn of the twentieth century as an act of imperialism by the US government. A comparison of Don Pedro's claims about what he called "Yanqui" imperialism with the more circumspect references to empire in the Apostle Paul's letters is instructive.

During his travels to Latin America in the late 1920s to explain the Puerto Rican situation, Albizu described an imperial agenda in US actions in Latin America for over a hundred years: "Puerto Rican Nationalism sustains that there exists more than a century of systematic imperialism by the United States directed, until recently, exclusively against Iberian-American nations, and presently, marching toward imposing a worldwide Yankee

---

4. The best accounts for the story of Pedro Albizu Campos are, of course, in Spanish, including essays and analysis by the Junta Pedro Albizu Campos (a cohort of Albizu historians), *Nervio y pulso del mundo*; Ayala Santiago, *Orden y Palabra en Los Discursos de Pedro Albizu Campos.*

hegemony."[5] Moreover, he continues, "the current military occupation of Puerto Rico is one of many instances of the North American imperial advance toward the South and this invasion should be seen in its global aspect as a continuous war against our nationalities."[6] Albizu references US action against Mexico in the 1840s and other such incursions, including the most recent ones (1898 and beyond) in the Caribbean. For Albizu, this imperial activity was not only a political and economic invasion but also a cultural and social one. For example, the act of imposing English-language instruction on Puerto Rican school children at the beginning of the imperial period was an act that guaranteed a generation of children with minimal education and little prospects for economic progress in the subsistence economy that resulted from US takeover of Puerto Rican farmlands.[7]

For Albizu and his cohorts in the Puerto Rican Nationalist movement what drove US imperialism was economics, backed by military force. Albizu argued that "the principles of [human] rights . . . have little influence on the imperialist soul: this one believes only in the force represented by wealth and the number of men at their disposal."[8] Albizu's conviction was based on the devastating impact of US economic interests, including private sugar corporations from the US, which had succeeded in converting previously successful, diverse cash crops for local Puerto Rican landowners, such as tobacco, coffee, pineapple, and other fruits, into mostly one—sugar cane—one that would be most lucrative for the US interests, but not local Puerto Rican farmers. Moreover, the US controlled exports and imports, such that local interests could not make shipping deals, for example, with any but US companies and at exorbitant costs. All of this and more had the devastating effect of enhancing the poverty and ill health of the average Puerto Rican on the Island. Puerto

5. Junta Pedro Albizu Campos, "Notas sobre el caso de Puerto Rico" in Albizu-Campos Meneses and León, *Albizu Campos: Escritos*, 1 (my translation). These "notes" were discovered in a Cuban archive in the 1970s. Laura Albizu-Campos was Albizu's wife. They met in Cambridge, Massachusetts, when Albizu was at Harvard Law School after 1916, and Laura Meneses, a Peruvian scientist, was doing post-doctoral studies at Radcliffe. After the death of Albizu in 1965, Dr. Meneses spent her later years in Cuba, where she died in 1973.

6. Albizu-Campos Meneses and León, *Albizu Campos: Escritos*, 1–2.

7. For a brief, but thorough, overview of the history of US colonialism in Puerto Rico, see Morales, *Fantasy Island*, 19–48.

8. Junta Pedro Albizu Campos, "La retirada americana de Santo Domingo," *El Nacionalista de Ponce*, Puerto Rico, July 13, 1925, reproduced in Albizu-Campos Meneses and León, *Albizu Campos Escritos*, 45 (my translation).

Rico had become a prime example of what one US economist of the time called "absentee capitalism," which left behind a "starving population" with resources drained "into the richest country."[9]

These dynamics of empire in the Puerto Rican story, with cultural and economic hegemony, argues Puerto Rican historian Mario Ayala Santiago, secured the "imposition of the North American Empire," which also "found insular associates" that helped install "a new colonial system."[10] Arguably, that "colonial system" stands to this day, evidenced by the terrible economic crisis in present-day Puerto Rico, exacerbated by devastating hurricanes in 2017 and 2022 and the ensuing infrastructure challenges on the Island. Unfortunately, but predictably, as a careful reading of Albizu shows, only US intervention can help fix these at this point in Puerto Rico's history. Moreover, such are the consequences of the US invasion of Puerto Rico in 1898 and its subsequent imperial presence.

Paul and Empire

Turning to a first-century CE apostle, Paul of Tarsus, we ask, "What did Paul say about "empire"? His most well-known statement is perhaps Rom 13:1–7, infamously used in recent years by the US Attorney General in the Trump administration to support family separation policies on the US border. It reads as follows (NRSV[11]):

> Let every person be subject to the governing authorities; for there is no authority except from God, and those authorities that exist have been instituted by God. Therefore, whoever resists authority resists what God has appointed, and those who resist will incur judgment. For rulers are not a terror to good conduct, but to bad. Do you wish to have no fear of the authority? Then do what is good, and you will receive its approval; for it is God's servant for your good. But if you do what is wrong, you should be afraid, for the authority does not bear the sword in vain! It is the servant of God to execute wrath on the wrongdoer. Therefore, one must be

9. For these and other details about US economic and military exploitation of Puerto Rico, see Denis, *War Against Puerto Rico*, especially 28–31. See also Juan Gonzalez, *Harvest of Empire*, 247–53.

10. Ayala Santiago, "Pedro Albizu Campos como punto de partida," in Junta Pedro Albizu Campos, *Nervio y pulso del mundo*, 27 (my translation).

11. Unless otherwise noted, all biblical references in this essay will use the New Revised Standard Version translation of the Bible.

subject, not only because of wrath but also because of conscience. For the same reason you also pay taxes, for the authorities are God's servants, busy with this very thing. Pay to all what is due them—taxes to whom taxes are due, revenue to whom revenue is due, respect to whom respect is due, honor to whom honor is due.

Neil Elliott, in his study of Paul's letter to the Romans, *The Arrogance of the Nations: Reading Romans in the Shadow of Empire*, includes among his list of features of empire the attempts to "win hearts and minds," namely through a propaganda project, as well as sheer military power.[12] Empires seek the "consent of conquered peoples" through both "violence and persuasion."[13] One aspect of Rome's imperial project was convincing the conquered that they could not rule themselves and needed the "benevolence" of Rome.[14] Rome claimed that the "*pax Romana*," achieved through violent military conquest, was a gift, nonetheless, to the universe, and only they, the proponents and keepers of the Roman imperial order, had the virtue and valor to secure and maintain for all the world to enjoy.

Moreover, Roman imperial hegemony was driven by economics in its search for conquest and colonization. As Elliott writes, "The costs of conquest were normally borne by the imperial treasury (meaning, by the slaves, peasants, and laborers who actually produced the wealth Rome appropriated through taxation), whereas the profits accrued to a small circle of wealthy and powerful individuals."[15] As a result, poverty and hunger abound among the heavily taxed peasant population and slaves. Elliott recounts numerous examples of how the imperial elite acknowledged the economic rape of their conquered masses. Such horrific treatment was only "natural," in the view of Roman senators like Cicero, who claimed, "liberty was the privilege of the imperial people" only and "their subjects had no inherent right to be free of Roman rule."[16] Such ancient imperial claims and assertions remind one of Pedro Albizu Campos's convictions about the rights and freedoms of the Puerto Rican people as a matter of natural law, self-determination, and human dignity, rather than control by an outside force like the US.[17]

12. Elliott, *Arrogance of the Nations*, 25–36.
13. Elliott, *Arrogance of the Nations*, 25–27.
14. Elliott, *Arrogance of the Nations*, 29.
15. Elliott, *Arrogance of the Nations*, 31.
16. Cited in Elliott, *Arrogance of the Nations*, 32.
17. See, for example, an analysis of Albizu's discussion of human rights in Ayala

Therefore, one wonders what Paul was arguing in writing these words in the latter part of his long letter to Roman Christ believers around the year 57 CE. Earlier in the letter, Paul seems to have urged non-Jewish and Jewish believers to see their faith in Christ as a justifying and reconciling force, not a divisive one (Rom 5:1–11). He calls upon them to live out their "baptism"—a sign of a new life in Christ, whether Jew or gentile (Rom 6:1–11). Not only is their life renewed in Christ, but it is also empowered by the Spirit of God, in the face of the imperial power that surrounds them and enslaves many of them. Paul writes at length in Rom 8:1–30 that in Christ there is no enslavement, but rather the power of the Spirit in each believer. Christ believers are not to be "conformed" to this "age," an *aiōni* controlled by empire. Rather, their "minds" are to be "renewed" and what is "good and acceptable and perfect" is not empire, but "the will of God" (Rom 12:1–2).

Yet, when Paul writes more explicitly about the Roman imperial order, he seems to support empire: "Let every person be subject to the governing authorities; for there is no authority except from God, and those authorities that exist have been instituted by God" (Rom 13:1). It seems that Paul was calling for practices that did not disturb the peace for Christ followers. As Elliott argues, throughout the letter to the Romans, Paul presents God as the arbiter of what is justice, not Rome. Yet, Rom 13:1–7 sounds too much like a prescription for letting any government do unjust things to its people. And certainly, that is how it has often been deployed, including in recent years during US anti-immigrant rhetoric.

However, to understand Paul more fully in this context, we need to look at what follows Rom 13:1–7, namely, 13:8–10 and 13:11–14:

> Owe no one anything, except to love one another; for the one who loves another has fulfilled the law. The commandments, "You shall not commit adultery; You shall not murder; You shall not steal; You shall not covet"; and any other commandment, are summed up in this word, "Love your neighbor as yourself." Love does no wrong to a neighbor; therefore, love is the fulfilling of the law. (Rom 13:8–10)

Paul seems to argue that despite what subjects of the empire might owe it, believers in Christ owe each other much more, namely, *love*.[18] Moreover,

---

Santiago, "Pedro Albizu Campos Como Punto de Partida," in Junta Pedro Albizu Campos, *Nervio y pulso del mundo*, 43–47.

18. So, Elliott, *Arrogance of the Nations*, 32. See also Rom 12:19–21 on principles of non-retaliation and "non-rivalrous love" (12:9; Elliott, *Arrogance of the Nations*, 224).

Paul continues, it is God who ultimately vindicates, not the empire, and *very soon*, he believed:

> Besides this, you know what time it is, how it is now the moment
> for you to wake from sleep. For salvation is nearer to us now than
> when we became believers; the night is far gone, the day is near.
> Let us then lay aside the works of darkness and put on the armor of
> light; let us live honorably as in the day, not in reveling and drunk-
> enness, not in debauchery and licentiousness, not in quarreling
> and jealousy. Instead, put on the Lord Jesus Christ, and make no
> provision for the flesh, to gratify its desires. (Rom 13:11–14)

Paul has no allusions to the "*pax Romana*," the rhetoric about "peace and security" that Rome supposedly brought to the nations, indeed through violence and force. Paul believed the empire to be temporary. So, non-resistance seems to be his answer in the letter to Roman Christ believers. They should practice "subjection" now to empire, as needed, but only as a temporary measure, for in due time all this is "passing away."[19]

There is, however, a problem in Paul's eschatological view in response to the empire. He himself often incorporates the language of empire and kyriarchy—"lordship"—to defend his apostolic authority within his communities. For example, in Paul's first letter to the Corinthians, some local leaders see themselves as exercising their freedom in Christ through prayer and preaching in public meetings of the Christ community. Paul, however, wants a cap on these public displays, especially as exercised by those who employ the gift of ecstatic speech ("speaking in tongues") and certain women prophets in the Corinthian community (see 1 Cor 11:2—14:40). Indeed, toward the end of this major section on spiritual gifts in the Corinthian assembly, Paul advises, "For God is a God not of disorder but of peace. As in all the churches of the saints, women should be silent in the churches. For they are not permitted to speak but should be subordinate, as the law also says. If there is anything they desire to know, let them ask their husbands at home. For it is shameful for a woman to speak in church. Or did the word of God originate with you? Or are you the only ones it has reached?" (1 Cor 14:33–36).[20] Although this directive is the third of a series

---

19. Elliot cites later Christian martyrs who took this passage to mean that obedience to empire had its limits; when the love of God's people and loyalty to God was challenged they must face the wrath of Rome, even though to their death they insisted no wrongdoing to "Caesar" even as they remained loyal to Christ. Even Paul, Elliott reminds us, was just such a martyr. Elliott, *Arrogance of the Nations*, 225–26.

20. There is ample debate about whether 1 Cor 14:34–36 was an interpolation added

of rebukes against speakers in the Christ assembly that speak "out of order" ("tongues-speaker," prophets, and certain women or wives), this still seems to be a stinging rebuke to women's agency in the Corinthian *ekklesia*, as Antoinette Clark Wire has shown in her important study, *The Corinthian Women Prophets.*[21] Earlier, in 1 Cor 11:2–16, Paul had argued from the rhetoric of the order of creation to similarly curtail women's leadership in the Corinthian community (by requiring that they wear head coverings during public, community worship if they are to pray or prophesy. Even so, there are indications in Paul's letters that women exercised leadership in the Pauline mission (e.g., Phoebe, an envoy from Paul to the Roman *ekklesiae*, according to Rom 16:1–2; Junia, referred to as an apostle in Rom 16:7; local leaders Euodia and Syntyche in the Philippian *ekklesia*, according to Phil 4:2–3). However, it seems that when Paul's apostolic authority was threatened, as in Corinth, he would re-inscribe *kyriarchy*—imperial, hierarchical language—to secure obedience in local communities, as argued by Elizabeth Schüssler Fiorenza.[22] Paul's eschatological vision and its urgency were also evident in these instances. A "soon return of Christ," he argued—the *Parousia*—necessitated members of the community to respond positively to his authority, just as it necessitated, especially among Roman Christians, practicing submission to the Roman imperial order.

Neil Elliott suggests that because the world of the Roman Empire had no real "unrestricted freedom," and no sense of "democracy, equality, and the rights of the individual," the Apostle Paul saw few options in helping his *ekklesiae* navigate those realities.[23] In contrast, in a different

---

by a later copyist, especially as influenced by a similar passage in the Paulinist letter, 1 Tim 2:9–15, where it is clear that the author wants to limit the role of women teachers and leaders in the community that receives 1 Timothy. See Horsley, *1 Corinthians,* 188–89, for arguments for interpolation of this text into the flow of the argument of 1 Cor 14, which seems contrary. However, see Odell-Scott, "Let the Women Speak in Church," 90–93, who argues *against* interpolation and believes this caution from Paul is directed at male hierarchical leadership in Corinth that would practice such limits to women's roles. That is, Paul was not making the directive; he was arguing against it, using the voice of his opponents to counter them. I also think the text is original to the letter, but believe that Paul is silencing "tongues-speakers," prophets that speak out of order in community assemblies, *and also* some women (wives?) who speak out of order.

21. Wire, *Corinthian Women Prophets.*

22. See Schüssler Fiorenza, *Power of the Word,* especially 1–109. She critically engages the more positive perspectives on "Paul and empire" found in such works as Horsley, *Paul and Empire* to suggest that Paul himself at times engages in the language of empire.

23. Elliott, *Arrogance of the Nations,* 56.

historical period, on the other side of the world, Pedro Albizu Campos, with his legal training and religious sensibilities toward human rights, saw clearly what was wrong with the US occupation of Puerto Rico, and demanded independence, nationhood, and freedom, even if it had to come through violent revolt. For Paul of Tarsus, ultimate freedom was in Christ, yet to be revealed in all its glory at the Return of Christ (Rom 13:11–14). In the meantime, "put on the Lord Jesus Christ," he told the Roman Christ assemblies, and "make no provisions for the flesh," that is, this life as we now know it because eschatological "salvation is nearer to us now than when we became believers" (13:11, 14). But it is *not* to be achieved in the "here and now," Paul seemed convinced. For Pedro Albizu Campos, the "here and now" was all we had, and independence and freedom were what Puerto Rico needed . . . now!

Citizenship: A Tool of Empire

A second feature I would like to explore in this essay comparing Paul and Pedro in light of empire is the issue of *citizenship*. In 1917, the Congress of the United States passed the Jones Act, which included two major pieces of legislation in Puerto Rico—US citizenship for residents of the Island, and limited shipping rules, with regard to whom the now US citizens of the Island could do business, i.e., no one but US interests. These strict limitations did not even allow ships from nearby Latin American nations to port in Puerto Rico, without traveling first to a US Southern port, unloading goods for reloading on a US ship. The costs of such machinations, of course, were untenable, and ultimately devastating for the Puerto Rican economy, with essentially only US companies as trading partners, on their terms. Precisely one hundred years later, in the aftermath of the horrific Hurricane Maria, these draconian shipping rules were suspended only briefly to allow for recovery assistance from Latin America and other places. Today those 1917 shipping rules are back in place, even as Puerto Rico faces tremendous economic challenges due to its other crisis besides Hurricane Maria in 2017, and then the more recent one—Fiona—in 2022: Predatory loans from US Wall Street interests to the Island's beleaguered government beginning in the early 2010s led to a prolonged debt crisis and bankruptcy for the Island. With regard to the latter, however, the Puerto Rican government, in fact, has no legal right to declare itself bankrupt! Such are the injustices of being a US colony for over 120 years.[24]

Pedro Albizu Campos, prophet as well as apostle, knew this would come. With regard to the other major stipulation of the Jones Act—US citizenship—Albizu argued that US citizenship for Puerto Ricans on the Island in fact denied the reality of *Puerto Rican* citizenship and, therefore, nationhood. When the US imposed its citizenship upon Puerto Ricans, it sealed its status as a colony, argued Albizu. "It is a denial of our natural citizenship," he wrote in 1930, and "our national personality."[25] US citizenship made Puerto Rican men eligible to be drafted to fight for the US in World War I, an obvious rationale for the inclusion of the citizenship stipulation in the 1917 Jones Act (the year in which the US entered the war already raging in Europe). But it also denied the fact of Puerto Rican natural citizenship and nationhood. Such is the force of empire, argued Albizu. Its encroachment on a free nation, he wrote, "atomizes the nationality of the occupied peoples." Granting citizenship to occupied peoples, rather than a sign of freedom, constricts them, argued Albizu, because it takes away that which is naturally theirs as a free nation. Only complete political independence restores that natural state of citizenship. Otherwise, Albizu concludes, "this colonization," under "this empire, the United States," has "wrested away our values."[26]

Paul and Citizenship

What did Paul say about citizenship? The book of Acts, written several decades after Paul's death, has Paul defending himself before a Roman tribunal by citing his Roman citizenship:

> But when they had tied him up with thongs, Paul said to the centurion who was standing by, "Is it legal for you to flog a Roman citizen who is uncondemned?" When the centurion heard that, he went to the tribune and said to him, "What are you about to do? This man is a Roman citizen." The tribune came and asked Paul, "Tell me, are you a Roman citizen?" And he said, "Yes." The tribune

24. For a thorough discussion of the impact of both Hurricane Maria and the debt crisis on Puerto Rico, see Morales, *Fantasy Island*, especially 49–252.

25. Albizu Campos, in Albizu Campos Meneses and León, *Albizu Campos: Escritos*, 73, my translation.

26. Albizu Campos Meneses and León, *Albizu Campos: Escritos*, 75, my translation.

answered, "It cost me a large sum of money to get my citizenship."
Paul said, "But I was born a citizen." Immediately those who were
about to examine him drew back from him, and the tribune also
was afraid, for he realized that Paul was a Roman citizen and that
he had bound him. (Acts 22:25–29)

As a result, Christian interpreters for centuries have suggested that Paul's
status as a Roman citizen, in accordance with the Acts narrative, facili-
tated his travels across the empire to bring good news about Christ to "the
nations."

Yet, Paul himself, in his letters, written mostly in the 50s CE, does not
discuss his citizenship status in the empire. After all, Roman citizenship
until the third century CE was difficult to come by; it usually depended
on birth and elite status, and could be purchased only by the most loyal,
well-to-do, and established families of the empire, whether in Italy or in
the colonies. That Paul never mentions it as a status he inherited or purchased probably means he did not have it. Moreover, when Paul does refer
to the status of Roman citizenship in general, he minimizes it, especially
in comparison to identity as a Christ believer. In Paul's letter to the Philippians, a Christ community in one of the most Rome-aligned cities in all of
Macedonia, Philippi, which coveted citizenship,[27] Paul writes,

> Brothers and sisters, join in imitating me, and observe those who
> live according to the example you have in us. For many live as
> enemies of the cross of Christ; I have often told you of them, and
> now I tell you even with tears. Their end is destruction; their god
> is the belly; and their glory is in their shame; their minds are set on
> earthly things. But our citizenship [politeuma] is in heaven, and it
> is from there that we are expecting a Savior, the Lord Jesus Christ.
> He will transform the body of our humiliation that it may be con-
> formed to the body of his glory, by the power that also enables him
> to make all things subject to himself. (Phil 3:17–21)

Again, as in the Rom 13 passage, Paul references his apocalyptic worldview when, apparently, some Christ believers in Philippi over-emphasize
Roman citizenship. Paul is trying to put the latter into an eschatological
perspective. In doing so, he suggests Roman citizenship is based on a system on its way out. In contrast, Christ believers will eventually experience a

27. See Philippi's historical and political alignments with Rome since Octavian (Au-
gustus) defeated Mark Antony there for full control of the empire, in O'Brien, *Commentary on Philippians*, 3–4. See also Bakirtzis and Koester, *Philippi at the Time of Paul
and After His Death*, 8–10.

more "glorious" citizenship that is heavenly and secured by God in Christ, to whom all will be ultimately "subjected," that is, not to the Roman Empire. Thus, Paul exalts a different kind of citizenship and thereby diminishes, at least before the eyes of his cohorts in the Christ *ekklesia*, Roman citizenship. Yet, this is not a major topic at all in most of the rest of the Pauline corpus, as it eventually becomes in the narrative about Paul, the second half of the book of Acts written, most likely, in the decade of the 80s CE. Interestingly, citizenship is a major topic for Pedro Albizu Campos centuries later, but only to *also* minimize it, especially because it had become a major benefit for the US presence on the Island. Citizenship was in fact a tool of empire, a matter of placating the residents of the Island and minimizing their self-identity, history, and culture. This brings me to a third and final topic of the comparison of Paul and Pedro for this essay, how empires "strike back" with imprisonment and violence in the face of opposition and resistance to imperial presence and power.

Imprisonment: Imperial Instrument of Silencing Resistance

Richard Cassidy, in a 2001 study, *Paul in Chains: Roman Imprisonment and the Letters of Paul*,[28] wrote extensively about Roman imprisonment and what might have been its impact on the Apostle Paul. By his own indication in his uncontested letters, Paul was imprisoned various times throughout his missionary travels (e.g., Phil 1:12–26; Phlm 1:1, 10, 22; 2 Cor 6:4–5; 11:23–33), and not just one final time in Rome. Cassidy shows the horrific physical setting and consistent threat of execution made Roman imprisonment a violent tool against any kind of resistance. Thus, wherever Paul was imprisoned, whether in the colonies during his travels or in the imperial capital at the end of his life, death was always around the corner of any Roman imperial cell.[29]

A passage from Paul's letter to the Philippians is again instructive here, as Paul describes his desire to return safely to the Philippian *ekklesia* one day:

28. Cassidy, *Paul in Chains*.

29. See Cassidy, *Paul in Chains*, especially 36–84, for treatment of prisoners under Roman rule in both colonies and imperial capital, including those arrested for *maiestas*—treason—as Cassidy argues Paul was for his preaching about another *kurios*—"lord"—not the emperor (he describes *maiestas* on 55–67 in particular).

For I know that through your prayers and the help of the Spirit of
Jesus Christ this will turn out for my deliverance. It is my eager
expectation and hope that I will not be put to shame in any way,
but that by my speaking with all boldness, Christ will be exalted
now as always in my body, whether by life or by death. For to me,
living is Christ and dying is gain. If I am to live in the flesh, that
means fruitful labor for me; and I do not know which I prefer. I
am hard pressed between the two: my desire is to depart and be
with Christ, for that is far better; but to remain in the flesh is more
necessary for you. Since I am convinced of this, I know that I will
remain and continue with all of you for your progress and joy in
faith, so that I may share abundantly in your boasting in Christ
Jesus when I come to you again. (Phil 1:19–26)

Just before this passage, Paul refers to his imprisonment (1:7, 12–18), but
we are not sure if it was his final imprisonment in Rome, or an earlier one.[30]
In any case, in Phil 1:19–26, Paul hopes for release and an apostolic visit to
Philippi. Despite the rhetoric of heavenly reward and its ultimate prefer-
ence, Paul makes the case for release from prison so he can visit his beloved
Philippian congregation. In doing so, Paul uses rhetorical *pathos* to make
an emphatic connection with the Philippian *ekklesia*: To die in Christ is
"gain," however, Paul would prefer to live and visit the Philippians: "To
remain in the flesh is necessary for you."[31] We do not know if Paul ever
did visit with the Philippians again. Moreover, the record is silent, even in
Acts, about when and how Paul finally died. Post-New Testament tradition
has him in a Roman prison, under guard, and then executed, perhaps by
Emperor Nero, sometime around 64 or 65 CE. But what actually happened
remains shrouded in mystery.[32]

30. Cassidy, *Paul in Chains*, 124–43, argues for Roman imprisonment, as does
O'Brien, *Commentary on Philippians*, 19–26. Koester, "Paul and Philippi," in Bakirtzis
and Koester, *Philippi at the Time of Paul*, argues for an earlier date for Philippians with
Ephesus as the location of imprisonment. Roetzel, *Letters of Paul*, 122–23, concurs, as
do I.

31. For introductory and specific textual studies of the rhetoric of *pathos* in Paul,
see Olbricht and Sumney, *Paul and Pathos*. Curiously, none of the essays in this volume
engages Paul's *pathos* of dying and living in Phil 1:19–26, although other aspects of Paul's
pathos in Philippians (namely in Phil 3 and 4) are referenced in Lauri Thurén, "'By Means
of Hyperbole' (1 Cor 12:31b)" in Olbricht and Sumney, *Paul and Pathos*, 97–113.

32. Scholars cite second and third-century references to Paul's Roman martyrdom
in the letters of Clement of Rome, the anonymous *Acts of Paul*, and Tertullian, among
others. For a good summary of these sources, see Goode, "Death of the Apostle Paul."
However, see Callahan, "Dead Paul," 67–84, for a careful analysis of these patristic texts

The Imprisonments of Pedro Albizu Campos

For Albizu Campos, two imprisonments, one in the 1940s in the US federal prison in Atlanta, and a final one in a Puerto Rican prison from 1950 to 1965 (except for a brief release in 1953) arguably took away the momentum for independence in Puerto Rico. In the 1930s, in particular, strong and positive progress toward independence ended with a long, first imprisonment. While in Atlanta, various US-based entities, including the American Civil Liberties Union, advocated for an early release. Due to illness while in Atlanta, Albizu was released under house arrest and taken to Columbus Hospital in New York. After his term was over, he spent a few additional years in New York, building up support for the Puerto Rican independence movement before returning to the Island in 1947.[33] Back on the Island, the effort to revive and organize for independence led to a violent revolt in November of 1950, which was immediately stopped by US and Puerto Rican forces. Thus, Albizu ended up in prison once again, this time in Puerto Rico. It led to illness, including a debilitating stroke in 1956, which literally silenced Albizu's voice.[34] He died in April 1965, shortly after being released by Governor Luis Muñoz Marin in late 1964.

In short, imprisonment has always been a tool of empire to control freedom fighters. While Pedro Albizu Campos clearly led a movement of liberation for political and cultural independence, we can ask ourselves about "the liberation movement" that the Apostle Paul led. Certainly, the first-century Christ movement, as understood and exercised by Paul of Tarsus was religious, apocalyptic, and eschatological. For Paul, the gospel movement could not go against the Roman Empire directly, because the latter's powers would only eventually yield, in his mind given his eschatological vision, to the divinely driven soon return of Christ. Rather, Paul argued that believers, until then, should receive the *spiritual* liberation available in Christ, and work to do good for each other, while waiting for God to

---

and the suggestion that the "trail" to Paul's death may have actually ended in Philippi and not Rome.

33. For correspondence from the ACLU, Dr. Laura Meneses de Albizu, and other supporters about the release of Albizu Campos and his fellow imprisoned Puerto Rican colleagues from the Atlanta federal prison in the 1940s, see the collection of letters in English and Spanish edited by Rosario Natal, *Albizu Campos*.

34. There were also accusations of experimental radiation by the US in the Puerto Rican prison, which debilitated Albizu Campos and left burn marks on his body, leading to the 1956 stroke. See, for example, the evidence described in Denis, *War Against All Puerto Ricans*, 233–45 (with photo on 236).

intervene in a final way, which would be the only way for believers to be ultimately liberated from imperial oppressive structures. In contrast, Pedro Albizu Campos, while a devout Roman Catholic, deployed his Caribbean-based Puerto Rican-defined Catholic faith toward action in the here and now; the eschaton was political liberation that needed to happen as soon as possible. Similar to Paul, he gave his life for that cause, although we cannot be certain when and how Paul died. We do know that Albizu died in April 1965, a few months after being released from prison in December 1964 by his old political counterpart, Governor Luis Munoz Marin. Pedro Albizu Campos had spent the larger part of 15 years (1950–1965) in a Puerto Rican prison for sedition against the United States of America (after having served a decade for a similar charge from 1937 to 1947).

Lessons from Putting Two Apostles in Conversation: Concluding Reflections

Defining Apostleship More Broadly

During a recent visit, I described to my Puerto Rican dentist, because he asked, some of my research comparing Puerto Rico's Pedro Albizu Campos and the New Testament's Paul of Tarsus as "apostles" from two different centuries. His response, in part, was, "But wasn't Paul a "saint"? I am sure he meant an official Roman Catholic "Saint," but I heard in his voice a concern that Pedro Albizu was not a "saint," but a problematic figure in Puerto Rican history. I gathered from our brief conversation that he did not much like talk about the independence movement or that part of Puerto Rico's history. I responded, "well, yes, he became a 'saint' in Roman Catholic tradition, but his initial designations included being an "apostle," which originally simply meant a missionary, a "sent one." In many ways too, I added, that is what Albizu was an itinerant preacher for the cause of Puerto Rican independence. Indeed, that's what "apostles" were—travelers across borders—whether Roman imperial borders in the case of Paul or Latin American borders in the case of Albizu. I have explored this notion further in my essay on Paul and migration, "Islands, Borders and Migration: Reading Paul in Light of the Crisis in Puerto Rico."[35] Broadly defined, apostles are travelers for a cause, usually across borders, whether physical or ideological. Certainly, both first-century Paul and twentieth-century Pedro were that.

35. Agosto, "Islands, Borders and Migration," 149–70.

Empires and Freedom

Empires are brutal. Beginning on February 24, 2022, we have seen that play out in horrific ways in the case of Russia's unwarranted attack on neighboring Ukraine. Russia's president, Vladimir Putin, wants to make Russia, once again, an imperial presence in Eastern Europe, and maybe beyond. Indeed, the categories of "empire" that play out across the centuries are often consistent. Authors Ashcroft, Griffiths, and Tiffin in *The Empire Writes Back: Theory and Practice in Postcolonial Literatures*, for example, cite the language of control and hegemony, such that language itself "becomes the medium through which a hierarchical structure of power is perpetuated." In such a dynamic, truth becomes restructured and realigned for the good of the empire to the detriment of the people. This study also asserts the reality of place and the *displacement* empires produce, as well as disorientation, alienation, and crisis in self-image, all of which result from colonization, enslavement, forced migration, refugee status, etc. These are the signposts of empire across the centuries.[36] They were evident in Paul's time, the Roman imperial order, and in Albizu's, the period of US hegemony over the Caribbean and Latin America in the late nineteenth century and throughout the twentieth. In my estimation, the US civil rights movement in the 1960s, and the development of liberation theology in Latin America and Black theology in this country, have helped mollify to some extent the imperial mindset and practices of nineteenth-century and twentieth-century US reality—notions about manifest destiny, for example, that Albizu references. It, however, rears its head regularly, as often as in the 1980s Reagan and recent Trump eras, especially with violent, virulent, anti-immigration rhetoric and policy engendered by US presidencies and political forces in particular. If US imperialism stopped a freedom movement in Puerto Rico dead in its tracks in the 1930s and then again in the 1950s, we need a strong progressive movement to stop right-wing white supremacy tendencies in our era, which also carry with them imperial, absolutist tendencies.

Lessons in Hermeneutics

Finally, as I close this essay, I want to share a word about the move in biblical hermeneutics that I make here and other studies on Pedro Albizu

---

36. Ashcroft et al., *Empire Writes Back*, 7.

Campos in comparison to the Apostle Paul.[37] How can I move across centuries with two very different people in two very different worlds, with arguably limited written evidence, much of which is actually rhetoric and oratory by the key figures, that is, Paul and Pedro? The reality is that I, as a Puerto Rican biblical scholar, cannot do anything *but* approach biblical and contemporary subjects in dialogue with each other. This was not the case more than three decades ago when I began this journey with traditional biblical training in graduate school. However, I think scholars like Elizabeth Schussler Fiorenza and Fernando Segovia, among many others, including those whose essays accompany mine in this volume, have been arguing for several decades now: Biblical scholarship must not avoid flesh and blood readers in an effort to practice a distancing, objectifying, exclusivist scientific exegesis.[38] The human and social justice dimensions—the "what for" and the "so what" of these exercises and research—must be part and parcel of our work, including biblical studies. If I am not taking my community—in my case, my Puerto Rican roots, religion, and history—into account, *para que*? For what? My context, my culture, and my person do and should dictate questions raised and directions taken. That, of course, is the heart of postcolonial biblical analysis, and I am indeed a child of a postcolonial reality, a reality, however, that is in many ways, still, a *colonial* reality when it comes to the Island of Puerto Rico. Therefore, I shall keep raising these kinds of questions and making these kinds of comparisons in the work that lies before me. And, of course, since this is still very much a work in progress, I invite the readers of this essay and this volume to provide input, questions, and challenges to the history, claims, and hermeneutics offered herein. In the words of scholars and followers of Pedro Albizu Campos everywhere, *¡Albizu sea!* (Loosely translated, "may the words and spirit of Albizu come alive.")[39]

37. Recent efforts in this regard include my two 2022 Croghan Bicentennial Lectures in Biblical Studies at Williams College: "The Apostle of Puerto Rican Independence: The Religion of Pedro Albizu Campos" (March 9, 2022) and "Colonized Apostles: Pedro and Pablo in Dialogue" (March 15, 2022). This current essay is a revision and expansion of the latter lecture.

38. Fernando F. Segovia made this critical point in his influential essay, Segovia, "'And They Began to Speak in Other Tongues,'" 1:1–32. Elizabeth Schüssler Fiorenza broke ground earlier in this regard with her 1987 Society of Biblical Literature Presidential addressed published as Schüssler Fiorenza, "Ethics of Biblical Interpretation," 3–17.

39. See, for example, the end of the opening two essays of Junta Pedro Albizu Campos, *Nervio y pulso del mundo,* 23 and 48, respectively.

PART II

Paul, Empire, and Race/Ethnicity

4

"Let This Mind Be in You"

Paul and the Politics of Identity in Philippians
—Empire, Ethnicity, and Justice

Demetrius K. Williams

When asked the question; which comes first, your race or your faith? I can answer without any hesitation. My faith of course! My identity as a Christian, triumphs over all possible intersection-alities I experience as a black woman. The matter of the soul is a matter much weightier; it surpasses and transcends the physical issues."—Giselle Agyare (2017)

"If I'm making any identity the core of who I am, once it gets attacked, I'm going to fall. But if my identity is in Christ, you can talk about my color, what kind of music I like, the things I affiliate with—and it won't affect me because that's not my rock, my foundation. If you talk about Christ, it still doesn't impact me because he's the only one of those things that won't fail."—Jeremiah Wright (2018)

"The message of 'social justice' diverts attention from Christ and the cross. It turns our hearts and minds from things above to things on this earth. It obscures the promise of forgiveness for hopeless sinners by telling people they are hapless victims of other people's misdeeds."—John MacArthur (2018)

THE STATEMENTS ABOVE WILL inform my reading and understanding of in-Christ identity in Phil 2:5–11, 3:1–11, and in the African American Christian experience wherein the unrelenting reach and unavoidable reality

43

of racism has complicated the quest for social and Christian-religious identity. The American empire having been constructed socially, culturally, religiously, and politically upon the erroneous notion and myth of race and blacks' biological inferiority, forcefully stripped, and significantly diminished many African descended peoples' concept of their identity forged in their original African socio-religious and cultural milieu. American enslavers, sanctioned and assisted by the emergent nation, continued a "re-narrativization" of African descended peoples that had begun earlier in Europe as biologically inferior black "heathens" and re-narrativized Europeans as biologically superior white Christians, utilizing the Bible and blacks' eventual incorporation into the Christian religion to shape a new identity for them as "slaves." The purpose of white Christian ministers' and missionaries' promotion of a proslavery in-Christ identity for enslaved blacks was to encourage passive acceptance of their "divinely sanctioned" subordinate status without recourse to legal or religious remedy—without recourse to seeking social justice. Despite the preaching of a skewed gospel sanctioning their enslavement, many enslaved blacks accepted the authority of the Bible and the Christian religion of their enslavers. Their Christianized descendants, however, must be wary of the "in-Christ identity" that white Evangelical preaching and teaching attempted to inculcate among their forbearers. In many ways, some white Evangelicals today, especially as represented by John MacArthur and his supporters, continue to promote an in-Christ identity hewn from the same stone of white proslavery preaching that seeks to discourage African American Christians from actively engaging the modern quest for social justice.[1] The two statements above by Giselle Agyare[2] and Jeremiah Wright[3] (not Jeremiah Wright Jr., pastor emeritus of Trinity Church of Christ, Chicago, IL) represents the subtle influence of in-Christ identity shaped by white evangelicalism: that is, for blacks to subordinate their ethnic birth identity beneath an in-Christ identity in such a way that diminishes the real and present racial concerns for social justice. It is important for African Americans to recognize that their own historic in-Christ

1. MacArthur and his supporters release a "Social Justice Statement" in 2018 that decried the contemporary social justice emphasis in Evangelical churches a heretical (along with Critical Race Theory). The statement was the result of a series of sermons MacArthur preached on "Social Justice and the Gospel."

2. Agyare, "My Race is a Part of my Identity but my Christian Faith Comes First."

3. Jeremiah Wright is an African American who serves as a staff minister at a predominantly white church (The Bridge Church). Wright, "Who You Are in Christ Changes Everything about Race."

identity that understood Jesus Christ as a liberator from both the spiritual oppression of evil and the social oppression slavery was forged through the flames of pervasive racism and persistent social-political injustice, which in many cases compelled them to press for freedom, dignity, equality, and social justice. They could not separate the value of their souls from the freedom of their bodies and their lived experience in the world.

The intent and purpose of this study is to interrogate and counter the current evangelical claims (held by many white and some black Evangelicals) that the Evangelical Church's support and promotion of social justice—indeed all Christian churches' quests in this regard—is not only misguided and contrary to the gospel, but also that such a mission-focus borders on heresy. Moreover, by implication African Americans' and many of their churches' historic quest for social justice is thereby misguided and heretical. Thus, African Americans are counselled, in essence, to be content with their white evangelically formulated in-Christ identity—an in-Christ identity which entails no social relevance or encouragement for social change. African Americans are also admonished to cease their "ethnic animus" that has been exacerbated by "playing the victim" (so-called victimology). This examination will argue that the African American quest for social justice is not only valid and necessary to challenge ongoing injustices and inequities, but also that such efforts pose no heretical threat to their in-Christ identity formed through their historic protest traditions. A brief overview of Phil 2:5–11 and 3:1–11 will begin our examination.

In-Christ Identity in Philippians

Paul's letter to the Philippians is written to a small Christ-believing gentile community that was "under the radar" of Roman imperial interest, insomuch as they maintained order and lived quietly. However, despite the frequent references to the letter as a "friendly letter," from what can be gleaned from a closer examination, there seems to be evidence of internal conflicts and external pressures that threaten the community's stability and unity.[4] This is most likely the reason that Paul attempted to root their communal identity in Christ Jesus through a compelling and evocative recounting of the hymn to Christ. To be sure, when Paul recounts the dramatic narratives of Christ in 2:6–11 and his own in 3:5–11, it seems apparent that his preoccupation in using these examples is to adjudicate an issue of identity that

4. Peterlin, *Paul's Letter to the Philippians in Light of Disunity in the Church.*

would strengthen internal unity against an external threat (Phil 1:27–30). He deploys the narratives of the Christ and himself to reorient the community to identify with a different set of religious values from both Judaism and Greco-Roman culture. This indicates that "identity politics" are in contention within this nascent community of Christ-followers in Philippi, a Roman colony. Paul engages a "politics of identity" in the Roman imperial realm that was taking place among the subject peoples of the empire that included the Judaism(s) of the day, and now also the Jesus-communities within his mission field.[5] Such a reading of the Christ-hymn in particular has only recently been undertaken[6] because Paul's language and rhetoric in Phil 2:5–11 and 3:5–11 have been read either doctrinally (i.e., "justification by faith" [3:8–10]) or theologically (esp. "Christ Hymn" [2:5–12]), which also includes the so-called "theological tendencies" of Paul's "opponents" (3:2, 18–19). When these passages are read through the lens of identity formation, different interpretive possibilities emerge.

I suggest that Paul offers his example in *Iudaismos* (Judaism, 3:4–12) before his encounter with Christ not as advocating a rejection of his Jewish birth ethnicity, but that his new ethnic identity in Christ did not require establishing a righteousness based upon the law (3:9) or circumcision (3:5)—the primary cipher and ethnic identity symbol of "Jewishness" in the ancient world.[7] This indicates that Paul (and later early Christian self-definition) recognized ethnic differences and engaged in "ethnic reasoning" to adjudicate in-Christ group identity.[8] Paul's statement, "For it is we are the circumcision, who worship in the Spirit of God and boast

5. Boyarin, *Radical Jew*; Esler, *Conflict and Identity in Romans*; Buell and Hodge, "Politics of Interpretation"; Hodge, *If Sons then Heirs*; Buell, *Why This New Race*; Sechrest, *Former Jew*; and Reese and Ybarrola, "Racial and Ethnic Identity," 65–82.

6. See Nebreda, *Christ Identity*. Nebreda offers a sustained focus on Phil 2:6–11 as a foundational narrative for social identity formation and explores the possible a/effects this has on the intended audience by a close reading of Paul's rhetoric.

7. Reese and Ybarrola make a similar point: " . . . one can hear the call to a new identity as the people of God, and such a call may mean giving up *controlling ethnic identities* as well as other identity markers, but there appear to be secondary ethnic and identity markers that still remain" (italics are mine). See Reese and Ybarrola, "Racial and Ethnic Identity," 73.

8. "Ethnic reasoning" refers to the ways that Christians defined themselves in terms of larger corporate collectives—"ethnic groups," "races," or "nations" (barbarians, gentile, Greek, Romans, Jew, Egyptian etc.[ix]) " . . . modes of persuasion Christians used to legitimize various forms of Christianness as universal, most authentic manifestation of humanity" and for determining insider/outsider affiliation and superiority (Buell, *Why This New Race*, 2). Buell also uses race and ethnicity used interchangeably (xi).

46

in Christ Jesus and have no confidence in the flesh" (3:3), means that he does not intend a radical break from his Israelite/Jewish *ethnic heritage* in Judaism: he is still part of the "circumcision"; however, it has now been newly conceived in Christ![9] This is how his narrative serves as a model for the Philippians to follow with respect to their *new identity* in Christ (2:5–11)—not allowing their righteousness to be based upon the law or circumcision (the primary ethnic Jewish religious symbol and identity marker) nor Roman imperial pagan religious practices to determine their in-Christ identity. Hence both the prototypical portrayal of the Christ and that of Paul serve to reinforce the Philippian community's *new identity* in Christ based upon his example and lordship to establish internal unity and reduce external threats. This seemingly minor shift in reading perspective offers insight for how the issue of in-Christ identity can be read in the African American Christian context.

The Christ-Hymn as a Foundational Narrative for Identity "In-Christ"

The Christ-hymn can be viewed as functioning both as a *prototypical model* for the Philippian community to emulate and as a *foundational narrative* for a new social identity.[10] As Paul employs it in his argument, it could be read as a veiled reflection and reference to their present social-political

9. Sechrest understands that Paul's new identity in Christ entails his incorporation into a new "race" (*genos*), which means that he no longer understood himself as a Jew within Judaism but as belonging to a new race in Christ. She argues that "Christian identity in Paul as one in which those who had been born Gentiles or Jews receive in Christ a new and separate ethno-racial identity." Furthermore, ". . . Pauline theology constructs a change in religious belief and practice as a change in ethno-racial identity . . ." (*Former Jew*, 5, 15, 210). I argue that even understanding himself to be a member of a new "race" (*genos*), Paul does not reject his Jewish/Israelite heritage. I suggest that Paul has a "hybrid" identity that has been "reconceived in Christ." His new in-Christ identity/"ethnicity" does not eliminate his understanding of himself as a Christ-believing "Jew" upon whom rests the promises of the messianic age that will welcome the Gentiles into the *commonwealth of Israel*. His new identity in Christ emphasizes a different basis for righteousness centered in Christ's death and resurrection, which makes possible Gentile incorporation into the religious heritage and promises of Israel fulfilling the promise to Abraham to be a "father of many nations."

10. Sechrest notes that Jews and Christians understood identity and their place in the world through religious meta-narrative (*Former Jew*, 4). To affirm in-Christ identity among the Philippians community is certainly one of the purposes for Paul's use of the Christ-hymn.

circumstances, especially in view of their current suffering as Jesus-followers within a pagan society (1:27–30). Traditional interpretations regarding the Christ-hymn have produced three schools of thought: 1) the *ethical*, 2) the *kerygmatic*, and 3) the *rhetorical* interpretations.[11] I suggest, however, that these lines of interpretation need not be read as mutually exclusive because each view offers insight into the probable function of the hymn. The ethical interpretation (dominant from the Reformers to the middle of the twentieth century) notes that verse 5 introduces the hymn by means of a syntactically problematic sentence, the translation of which has great bearing on the interpretation. The main thrust of this view is that the experience of Jesus Christ characterized by humility and self-sacrifice in verses 6–8 serves as an *ethical example* or *model* for the Philippians to observe and to imitate. Christ's exaltation as "Lord" (vv. 9–11) is not presented for imitation but to offer the assurance that they can share in his glory (the transformation of their lowly bodies as in 3:20–21) in the eschaton when he is seated in glory. The ethical interpretation, then, supplies the verb "to be" to verse 5b. Thus, Paul presents the example of Christ as a way of life characterized by a willing adoption of a lower status and identity of humility and self-sacrifice: a disposition that should be adopted among the Philippians. The connection between Paul's exhortation to the Philippians for self-sacrificial humility (vv. 1–4) and that of Christ's humility and sacrifice in the hymn (vv. 6–8) is joined by verse 5 translated as: "Adopt towards one another, in your mutual relations, the same attitude that was found in Christ Jesus."[12] Inferred in this interpretation is the addition, *to phronema* ("attitude" or "frame of mind"), which has been described in verses 1–4 and which is the direct object of *phroneite*.[13] This is the hinge for the ethical interpretation. This interpretation of the Christ-hymn, however, is problematic for imitation in African American Christian context because it encourages Christians to willingly submit to suffering and humiliation in imitation of the Christ portrayed in the hymn who was "obedient" unto death, which was encouraged and expected of enslaved blacks in antebellum America.

The *kerygmatic* interpretation that emerged during the 1950s argues that Paul quotes the hymn to remind the Philippians of *how they came to*

---

11. See Williams, "Philippians," 482–89.

12. Moule, "Further Reflections on Philippians 2:5–11," 265.

13. O'Brien, *Philippians*, 254.

be "in Christ."[14] This line of interpretation proposes the following translation: "adopt towards one another, in your mutual relations, the same attitude as you adopt towards Christ Jesus, *in your union with him*" (my emphasis).[15] Furthermore, it is proposed that the phrase "in Christ Jesus" (*en Christo Iesou*) represents a technical theological formulation in Paul that refers to the union of believers with Christ. Therefore, the expression points to the *salvation event*, not a piece of teaching on Christ's ethical example, or even a discussion of Christ's relationship to God.[16] While I am sympathetic to this line of interpretation because it avoids promoting notions of innocent suffering, it overlooks too forcefully the ethical and full rhetorical thrust of Paul's argument.

The important aspect of the rhetorical interpretation is that it captures the function of the hymn and its language in its connection to Paul's use of examples in the letter. The examples are those of Christ (2:6–11), Timothy (2:19–24—who has genuine concern for their welfare not looking out for his own interests), Epaphroditus (2:25–30—who served on the Philippian's behalf and became ill almost "unto death"), his own (3:1–11, who willing relinquished privilege of status like Christ [suffered the "loss of all things"]), and the Philippian community (4:10–20—who formed a partnership with Paul sacrificially sharing of their resources). The negative examples are represented by Paul's rivals who preach out of selfish ambition (1:15–18), those who promote circumcision (3:1–3, 18–19), and Euodia and Syntyche (4:2–3).[17] All of these examples demonstrate that Paul's primary objective in using the hymn is not only to explain how the community of believers came to be in union with Christ. He also sought to encourage an "attitude" and *praxis* among them that was exemplified in Jesus Christ "who emptied himself" of privilege and status, a paradigm that Paul seeks to establish as a model for mutual relations in the community.[18] The exhortation for the

14. See Martin, *Carmen Christi*, 71; Ernst Käsemann ("Critical Analysis," 83–84).

15. Käsemann remarks that, "The Philippians are admonished to conduct themselves toward one another as is fitting within the realm of Christ" ("Critical Analysis," 84).

16. Käsemann, "Critical Analysis," 84.

17. See Kittredge, *Community and Authority*, 90–100. She offers an insightful analysis of the Euodia and Syntyche examples.

18. I agree with Reese and Ybarrola who state: "The language of the New Testament locates Christians within a new family, a family with God as its head and with relationship in Christ as its main location. And this new familial and thus ethnic identity is to shape the behavior of Christians to be a certain type of people." See Reese and Ybarrola, "Racial and Ethnic Identity," 72. That type is modeled on the example of Christ.

compatible attitude in 2:1–4 precedes the various examples of the *practical behavior* exemplified in the hymn. Moreover, the opening imperative in verse 5 provides a transition from verses 1–4 to verses 6–8 (9–11) and demonstrates that Christ's example that follows is *intentionally paradigmatic*.[19] Therefore, to drive a wedge between verses 4 and 5 and to separate verses 1–4 from what follows in verses 6–11 is confusing. It is apparent then that verse 5 is an important transitional sentence that links the exhortations (of vv. 1–4) to the Christ-hymn.[20] In view of this, the interpretations should not be understood as an "either or" function of the hymn but as "both and." Paul employs the Christ-hymn to portray both the Philippians' "*union with/how they came to be* in Christ Jesus" and the kind of commensurate behavior that is in keeping with Christ's attitude and example. Thus, the hymn functions not only as a kerygmatic reminder of how they came to be "in Christ," but also as governing metaphor[21] or paradigm for the community to emulate as demonstrated through the examples. This forms the basis of their new social identity in Christ constructed in contention with both Judaism and Roman pagan imperialism. Recognizing the mutual functions of the ethical, kerygmatic, and rhetorical interpretations in the construction of in-Christ identity is instructive for understanding Paul's account of his example in 3:1–11 formed in contention with his former life in Judaism.

Paul the Prototype of in-Christ Identity

If the Christ-hymn served as a paradigmatic or prototypical model for in-Christ identity for the Philippian believers, then it is possible to understand Paul's account in Phil 3:1–11 as a personal example or prototype of one who has already made the transition to identity in Christ. When Paul states in verse 3 that "We are the circumcision . . . " (i.e., those who have been united in Christ), he is not only spiritually reevaluating the identity marker of "circumcision" as belonging to the newly reconstituted in-Christ community composed of both Jew and gentile as the people of God, but also portraying

19. For Fee, Paul's point seems plain enough. He begins with an emphatic "this," which is best understood as pointing backward, in this case to verses 2–4. That is followed immediately by the imperative, "this think," which purposely harks back to verse 2 (*phroneite/phronountes*). Thus the basic imperative sums up the whole of verses 2–4: "This mindset (i.e., that which I have just described) have among yourselves." Fee, *Philippians*, 200.

20. O'Brien, *Philippians*, 205.

21. Perkins, "Heavenly Polituema," 103.

how his new "ethnoracial"[22] identity contrasts with his old identity. Verse 4 serves as a transitional clause (like that of 2:5 introducing the Christ-hymn) that facilitates the transition to Paul's account of his former status and identity under the law in Judaism, which is composed of four items that he possessed by virtue of his ethnic-religious heritage: "circumcised on the eighth day, from the people (*genos*) Israel,[23] tribe of Benjamin, a Hebrew from Hebrews" (v. 5). The last three items he mentions are those that he accomplished on his own merit: "according to the law, a Pharisee; according to zeal, persecuting the church; according to righteousness which is in the law, blameless" (v. 6). All the things that he mentions in verses 4–6 represented his previous identity markers and privilege of status under the law and as a part of the "circumcision" (Judaism) before his encounter with the Christ.

Paul proceeds from this point to give an account of his new status and identity in Christ through the language of the "loss of worth" of his former values and status, which now are to be found in "gaining Christ" (being in Christ). Paul explains in verses 7–8 that he came to view his previous confidence and status as a member of the "circumcised" under the law as having lost their worth. What Paul regarded before as success and accomplishment, even a basis of righteousness before God, he now considers devoid of value. These are all ways of expressing that his and the Philippians' future advantage lie in "gaining" and being "in Christ" without recourse to the identity markers of circumcision and righteousness based upon the law.[24] If his former strivings are the Philippians' present goals—to accept law keeping and circumcision, an identity marker in Judaism—, then they too are driven toward that which is "confidence in the flesh" (v. 4). In verse 9 Paul addresses *righteousness* and *faith*, the foundation of his present code of values and in-Christ identity. Now in verses 9–11 Paul will focus exclusively on the positive side. The very things he once regarded as failure, worthless,

22. "Ethnoracial" indicates a blend of continuity and discontinuity between ancient and modern constructs of race and ethnicity. See Buell, "Rethinking the Relevance of Race for early Christian Self-definition," 450n3.

23. See Buell and Hodge, "Politics of Interpretation." They point out that differences between ancient and modern concepts of race: 1) *genos* often deemed to be produced and indicated by religious practices; 2) ethnicity was viewed as mutable (despite a frequent correlation between ethnicity and physical descent). Religion produced race in antiquity (Buell, *Why This New Race*, ix–x).

24. See Braxton, *No Longer Slaves*. He argues that Paul is sympathetic to Jewish culture aside from specific boundary marker practices and strongly rejects any efforts to force gentiles to adopt a Jewish ethnic identity as a condition of conversion. See also Sechrest, *Former Jew*, 8–9.

and indeed contrary to the law and circumcision, he now acknowledges and recognizes to be the only goal worth pursuing—that is, being found righteous before God "in Christ" and having the knowledge of Jesus as Lord and sharing in the likeness of his death and resurrection (vv. 9–11). To be sure, this is the basis of his new identity "in Christ"! This is the source of his and the Philippian in-Christ-group identity that can be seen even more clearly by comparing his narrative with that of the Christ hymn.

Paul's narrative account indicates that his own life and apostolic career is homologous with the crucifixion/resurrection pattern.[25] In Phil 3:4–11, whose striking reversal recalls that of the Christ hymn (2:6–11), Paul describes his own "self-emptying" in order to identify with the *kenosis* of Christ.[26] This can be seen in the way he presents his own example in terms of the privilege he had as an ethnic Jew in Judaism and the voluntary loss-of-privilege pattern that is analogous to that expressed in the Christ hymn (Phil 2:6–11, esp. vv. 6–8). For this reason, Wayne Meeks suggests that the hymn serves as a *master model* for Paul's own narrative paradigm. He states:

> . . . the hymn's story of Christ is the master model that underlies Paul's characterization of his career . . . . This model sets the terms of the thinking and acting expected of the Philippians in the face of conflict inside and hostility from outside the community. It is within this larger context, the controlling structure of the whole letter, that we should understand the specific verbal connections between the hymn and the immediate parenetic context.[27]

Paul's abandonment of the *privileges* of his Jewish heritage to "know Christ" and find a righteousness based on faith in Christ is portrayed as abandoning a position of "earthly" status.[28] Now he awaits the resurrection (exaltation, 3:11), which will be gained through his participation in and identification with the Christ (3:10–11) who also willingly forsook his divine privilege (2:6–8) to identify with those who needed the embrace of God's justice (righteousness). The connection with the Christ hymn is also confirmed by some explicit verbal parallels: 1) "reckon/consider (2:6; 3:7–8); 2) "form" (2:7; 3:10); 3) "to find" (2:7; 3:9); 4) "Lord" (2:11; 3:8). In both the narratives of Christ and Paul the *reversal* pattern of God's actions

---

25. Meeks, *First Urban Christians*, 181.

26. Collange, *L'Epître de Saint Paul aux Philippiens*, 128.

27. Meeks, "Man from Heaven," 335.

28. Gnilka, *Philipperbrief*, 186–89.

can be seen.[29] This pattern of reversal is an important element of Paul's narrative strategy, which indicates to his intended audience that his own participation in the prototypical example of Christ allows him (and other believers) to participate in the reversal pattern of God's divine activity. For this very reason Paul uses his example as a prototypical model of one who within *Iudaismos* (Judaism) has appropriated *a new identity* "in Christ" (3:4–11). Philippian Christ-followers are encouraged to follow Paul's example (3:17) in terms of their own experience of a new identity "in Christ" (2:6–11) vis-à-vis their social situation in Greco-Roman political-religious traditions and values. N.T. Wright argues that "Paul is using here warnings against the former (Judaism) as a code for warnings against the latter (Roman pagan imperialism). But his method of warning them, and of encouraging them to take a stand for the counterempire of Jesus, is given for the most part in code."[30] This has both social and political implications for the Philippian community.

Politically, the Christ hymn provides the theological bases for renouncing one's real or imagined claims or hopes of attaining status and privileges in the Roman *imperium*. And instead, not identifying the exalted Caesar of Rome but with the humble Christ of the narrative who is soon to return as savior and lord of the heavenly commonwealth.[31] Politically, then, the Philippian Christ-followers are to see themselves as belonging to a different commonwealth (*politeuma*, 3:20; also 1:27, *politeuestha*), a heavenly *politeuma* with a different Lord and polity. Therefore, they are to reject "invitations . . . to seek a special status through membership in a substitute, earthly society."[32] The social implications of the Christ hymn emerge as Paul exhorts the Philippian community to seek the model of behavior and frame of mind exhibited in the new reality in Christ: "since Christ rejected equality with God [*isa Theou*] for the slave-like humiliation *of the cross*, all forms of human status and every attempt to secure one's social or religious position by gaining social status is rejected."[33] Thus the "death on the cross" makes Christ a different kind of *savior* than the

---

29. Perkins states: "The Christ hymn shows the status reversal of Christ over the powers of the kosmos (from slave to Lord)." See Perkins, "Christology," 513. Cf. Phil 2:1–11; Rom 15:1–3; 1 Cor 1:18—2:5; 2 Cor 8:9, 13:4; Gal 6:2.

30. Wright, *Paul's Gospel*, 174–75.

31. Perkins, "Heavenly Polituema," 95–98.

32. Perkins, "Heavenly Polituema," 108.

33. Perkins, "Heavenly Polituema," 103 (my emphasis).

Caesar of the Philippian Christians' civic experiences. Ben Witherington makes this point even more emphatically:

> The language of boasting and honor in this passage reminds us that the Greco-Roman world had one set of values as to what amounted to honorable and shameful behavior and the Christian communities had another, though clearly there was some overlap. In a Roman setting like Philippi, honor was bound up with the public order, the doing of public works, and the behavior that bolstered the values of society and brought society's acclaim. Paul is trying in part in this discourse to de-enculturate his audience from such values by indicating that they are part of a different commonwealth, holding a different sort of citizenship; he thus uses different examples of what amounts to honorable or shameful behavior. The model for their behavior is not Caesar, with his displays of military power and public games, but Christ, who takes on the form of a slave (see Phil. 2). It needs to be understood that humility and servant-like behavior were not generally seen in the Greco-Roman world as admirable or even honorable, but rather in many cases were viewed as despicable and improper for a free person, especially a Roman citizen. For Paul, however, the pattern of Christ's life, as encapsulated in the Christ hymn in Philippians 2, was also the pattern for ministry and for Christian life in general, i.e., self-chosen servanthood, followed by exaltation.[34]

What this means is that the Christ hymn that portrays a humble and self-giving example of Christ was to provide the communal ethos and nature of in-Christ identity as a counter to the values of Greco-Roman society, which extolled the quest for status, competition, and privilege. Paul's examples of rivalry, competition, self-centered attitudes, and self-seeking motivations are the primary examples of such. Paul uses his own story of how he had abandoned his *status* and *privileges* in Judaism for a new identity in Christ, to encourage the Philippians to imitate and identify with his example (3:17) in light of their social and religious context. His example indicates that identity in Christ obliterates any human group's racial-ethnic identity (and identity markers) *as a basis* for establishing in-Christ identity for all Christians.[35] Christ is the only foundation upon

34. Witherington, *Friendship*, 47–48.

35. This point is different from Daniel Boyarin who argues that Paul's supersessionist theology obliterates the legitimacy of racial and ethnic difference (esp. Jewish difference) normalizing a single identity that became white, male, and European. Boyarin, *Radical Jew*. See also Sechrest, *Radical Jew*, 8.

which to build the universal identity of the community (as in the Christ hymn but also see 1 Cor 3:11–15). Paul's narrative is shaped in contention with Judaism to show that birth descent and religious identity exemplified by "circumcision" cannot form the basis of in-Christ identity for the gentiles. Identity in Christ for ethnic Jews and gentiles is founded upon faith in the sacrificial death of Christ on the cross that brings about a new standard of righteousness and relationship with God, which is no longer based upon birth descent. The point is that no group's ethno-racial identity (and associated markers) should form the basis of a "universal" in-Christ identity. And while the racial-ethnic birth identity of Jews and gentiles in Christ is not eliminated, it still cannot form the universal basis of in-Christ identity. How might the example of Christ in Phil 2:5–11 and Paul's example in 3:1–11 offer insight into African American Christian religious experience? What might be gleaned by examining how socio-religious and political forces in the American empire influenced and impinge upon their Christian religious identity?

Philippians 2:5–11 and in-Christ Identity in the North American Historical Context

In the historical America context, it is evident that Christians of ethnic European descent did the very thing that Paul denounced: they created an in-Christ identity for universal Christendom not based upon the foundation and example of Christ in the hymn but based upon a newly constructed ethno-racial identity as "white." The emergent national identity and Christian identity, moreover, merged with "whiteness" to construct a system of slavery that would be compatible with Christianity and the nation's democracy.[36] This effort corrupted Christianity's essential values and made the nation's government a mockery of democratic principles. The merging of Christian identity with whiteness began with the colonization and occupation of New World territories and the domination of their inhabitants, along with the importation of enslaved Africans to the various colonies and Islands in the Caribbean. Colonization and enslavement of other human beings were initially justified on the grounds that their goal was to "save their souls." This "New World" colonizing and enslavement venture under the guise of evangelism justified both the seizure of native/indigenous lands and the enslavement of black Africans.

36. Daniels, *White Lies*, 41.

Recognizing that the early church not only accepted slavery, but also preached along with the theoretical support of Aristotle that enslavement could be *spiritually advantageous*,[37] Catholic and Protestant theologians perceived a powerful paradigm for constructing the "in-Christ identity" of subjugated and enslaved peoples using the Christ hymn. They could argue that even Jesus Christ, the Son of God, was crucified as the ultimate *obedient slave* when "he made himself nothing by taking the very nature of a *servant*" (*doulos*, literally "slave" in Greek).[38] And being found in appearance as a man, he humbled himself by becoming *obedient to death*—even death on a cross" (Phil 2:7–8 NRSV). But crucifixion and death were not the ultimate end for the Christ. Because of his steadfast obedience to God in facing the suffering, degradation, and humility of the cross, he was resurrected, exalted, and enthroned in the heavens:

> Therefore God exalted him to the highest place and gave him the name that is above every name, that at the name of Jesus every knee should bow, in heaven and on earth and under the earth, and every tongue acknowledge that Jesus Christ is Lord, to the glory of God the Father. (Phil 3:9–11 NRSV)

The one who died an ignominious death on a Roman cross as God's deliverer, who identified with the poor, the outcast, and the marginalized, and even took on the "very nature of a slave" and was exalted in heaven, seated on a throne, and given the name (title) that is above every name, "Lord" (*kyrios*) because of his obedience to God as a faithful "slave" (*doulos*). The crucifixion is the narrative dividing line in the Christ hymn between the Christ as *doulos* who is powerless (or empties himself of power) and humbly acquiesces to his suffering, and the Christ as *kyrios* before whom all bow to his magisterial power as sovereign Lord. This early Christian hymn[39] conceptually divides into two different christological portraits separated by the crucifixion, but both of which would become ideal for serving the prerogatives of empire: an exalted Christ (*kyrios*) for rulers and

---

37. See Gerbner, *Christian Slavery*, 15; Blackburn, *Making of New World Slavery*, 36; Glancy, *Slavery in Early Christianity*.

38. Mitzi J. Smith suggests that there is a strong probability that the *doulos* reference in Philippians is more than metaphorical in as much as it is used in reference to Mary in Luke. See, "Abolitionist Messiah," 53–70.

39. For Paul's rhetorical use of this "hymn" to Christ see Williams, "*Enemies of the Cross of Christ*."

the powerful of empire, and a humiliated/obedient Christ (*doulos*) for the enslaved and subjugated peoples of empire.

Using the Christ hymn as a paradigm for supporting slavery and white supremacy, Protestant missionaries and preachers formulated a christological model to nurture a pedagogy of passivity among enslaved blacks that would be useful in their aim to inculcate within them a sense of resignation and acceptance of their "God-given" place, purpose, and destiny—their lot in life as slaves in perpetuity. They also created a version of Christianity that they hoped would also be more acceptable to the proslavery prerogatives of the planter class. This version of Christianity, if preached, taught, and propagated "properly," would make enslaved blacks more pliable, passive, and profitable. Winthrop Jordan offers a telling assessment of this approach to propagating the gospel, stating that: "These clergy men had been forced by the circumstance of racial slavery in America into propagating the Gospel by presenting it as an attractive device for slave control."[40] They believed that the paradigm of the Christ hymn would serve as an ideal model for the religious pedagogy of enslaved blacks and ensure the social stability of the Southern slave regime. Their emphasis is significantly on Jesus Christ as the ultimate *obedient slave* who "made himself nothing by taking the very nature of a *slave*" and "humbled himself by becoming *obedient to death*—even death on a cross" (Phil 2:7–8). This is "the mind of Christ" that the antebellum Southern preachers and missionaries sought to inculcate within the enslaved black population (Phil 2:5). The second half of the christological narrative that develops after the cross/crucifixion (which is the dividing point in the narrative) is depicted in Phil 2:9–11 where Christ is exalted and declared "Lord" to whom all solemnly bow in reverence. This second narrative portion of the Christ hymn reflects Jesus Christ as the "Compassionate Heavenly Slave/Master" in whose guise one finds the benevolent earthly "master" or planter. This proslavery Christ could adequately assume the role of "slave/master" because he is the master (*kyrios*) that had also been an obedient slave (*doulos*), and as such, he is sufficiently capable of modeling the proper deportment and providing appropriate instruction to both "slave" and "master." Thus, the preaching and teaching of the Compassionate Heavenly Christ as "Slave/Master" is "the mind of Christ" that preachers and missionaries wanted to nurture within the white planter class. The powerful Christology depicted in Phil 2:5–11 would serve well

---

40. Raboteau, *Slave Religion*, 103; Jordan, *White Over Black*, 192.

the purposes of the powerful and the prerogatives of proslavery preaching and teaching in the American South.

Jesus Christ was one with whom the enslaved could identify because he himself became an obedient servant (slave), and in so doing, proslavery preachers and missionaries could portray Jesus as the exemplary "servant-of-servants. The portrayal of Jesus Christ as the "servant-of-servants" refers directly to the Christology of Phil 2:5–8 and the Curse of Ham (actually Canaan) in Gen 9:25 where the language of "servant of servants" is found. This combination of texts was certainly in the mind of Bishop William Meade (Assistant Bishop of Virginia) in his *Pastoral Letter* (1834) written "To the Members, Ministers and Friends of the Protestant Episcopal Church in the Diocese of Virginia." He composed this letter that included the subtitle, "[O]n the Duty of Affording Religious Instruction to Those in Bondage," to impress upon the planter class their responsibility of allowing religious instruction to the enslaved. Meade states in this regard: "This gospel was preached to the poor. How exactly was it suited to all their needs. To recommend it the more, and secure the reception of it, our glorious Emmanuel *chose the form of a servant, became the servant of servants*, illustrating its blessed doctrines by his own meek, patient, suffering life"[41] (emphasis added). Meade is certainly referring to Phil 2:7 ("but made himself of no reputation, and took upon him the *form of a servant* [*slave*]") when he states that Jesus Christ "chose the form of a servant" and suggested that his earthly life exemplified this reality through his "meek, patient, suffering life." The decision of the Christ to become a "servant" to the *poor* (the term he uses to allude to enslaved blacks and other oppressed, peoples) according to Meade, was providential and built into the very essence of the gospel. However, the "gospel to the poor" has become deradicalized and disempowered from its prophetic moorings in Meade and other proslavery preachers! In Isaiah, as in Luke, the "good news to the poor" portends a radical reversal of social relations where the poor take center stage in God's messianic intervention and transformation of society! Justice will reign and Jubilee will prevail for the poor and oppressed. Not so in proslavery preaching and propaganda. More importantly, we must ask how is Meade using Gen 9:25 to advance his argument about Jesus as the servant-of-servants? It appears that he is relating the servanthood of Christ directly to the so-called "Curse of Ham" and the *presumed* perpetual enslavement of blacks, which is erroneously founded upon this passage! The text says that *Canaan* shall be a "servant of

41. Meade, *Pastoral Letter*, 11.

servants" to his brothers. If Meade is reading Phil 2:6–8 through the lens of Gen 9:25, it is possible to surmise that for him the servanthood of Christ is a uniquely designed christological paradigm for justifying the enslavement of blacks who share with Christ the role of obedient servant-of-servants. White ministers frequently employed the hermeneutics of sacrifice and servitude in their proslavery arguments."[42] Moreover, although Christ himself is identified with the "Curse of Ham" as a "servant-of-servants" by astoundingly submitting to the form of a slave (*doulos*) himself, his purpose was not to liberate blacks from slavery or the presumed curse. His role, on the contrary, was to provide a paradigm or model for the enslaved to follow, demonstrating how to *fulfill the role* of an *obedient slave* that, in pro-slavery propaganda, would be pleasing to God. Meade's exegesis represents the lengths to which proslavery preaching and interpretation would go to justify their ideological claims of black enslavement.

As Meade continues his pastoral advice, he observes that Jesus's life and teachings are designed particularly to pacify the poor and provide a paradigm for the enslaved to follow in order to ensure that they will find contentment in life, reducing the threat of rebellion. He continues, "How he adapted all his precepts and promises and doctrines to the poor, and those who are in bondage. Where will you find a word that proceeded from his lips, which could excite pride, discontent or rebellion."[43] For him and other proslavery preachers the gospel of Jesus Christ was designed from its inception to simply "save souls" and to domesticate the enslaved and oppressed to uphold the status quo. With the Christology of Jesus Christ as the "servant-of-servants" buttressed with New Testament passages on the duty of slaves to their earthly masters and vice versa, proslavery preachers could declare that "this Jesus founded a religion that was 'the pillar' of society, the safeguard of nations, the parent of social morals, which alone has the power to curb the fury passions, and secure everyone his right."[44] Riggins Earl calls this Jesus a "law-and-order Jesus" who blesses "the social order to the rich, the enjoyment of their wealth; to the nobles, the preservation of their honors; and to the princes, the stability of their thrones."[45] The Jesus of this christological paradigm was indisputably opposed to the instability of society, to insurrection, anarchy, bloodshed or revolts against

---

42. Copeland, *Knowing Christ Crucified*, 11.

43. Meade, *Pastoral Letter*, 11.

44. Earl, *Dark Symbols*, 37–38.

45. Earl, *Dark Symbols*, 38.

the "masters," treason or sedition against states, which is the stark opposite of the Jesus of the Gospels who came to turn social order on its head ("Do not think that I have come to bring peace to the earth; I have not come to bring peace, but a sword." [Matt 10:43 NRSV]).

Rev. James Henley Thornwell was considered the most competent and articulate theologian of the antebellum South. He was a major proponent of the "spirituality of the church" doctrine. Thornwell proposed that since the Bible is the church's "Constitution" and the church has no jurisdiction over political and social matters, "the power of the church is only ministerial and declarative."[46] The church must, therefore, be silent on those matters which the Bible is silent. Hence, the church "has no commission to construct so-ciety afresh . . . to re-arrange the distribution of its classes, or to change the form its political institutions."[47] In short, the church, as an institution, must remain silent on the most pressing ethical and decisive moral, social, and political questions of the day—in his day that pressing moral, social and pollical issue was slavery. The most articulate white Evangelical Chris-tian theologian of the day counselled the church to remain silent on this pressing social justice issue. Not surprisingly, he also makes the proslavery Christology of a passive, obedient, status quo Jesus the pillar of white soci-ety in his sermon "The Rights and Duties of Masters" when he asserts:

> Insurrection, anarchy and bloodshed—revolt against masters, or treason against states, were never learned in the school of Him [the proslavery Christ], whose Apostles enjoined subjection to the magistrate, and obedience to all lawful authority, as characteristic duties of the faithful. . . . Christian knowledge inculcates content-ment with our lot.... It subdues those passions and prejudices, from which all real danger to the social economy springs. . . . Christian knowledge softens and subdues.[48]

Enslaved blacks were admonished to imitate in their own conduct and lives this "non-threatening" status quo portrayal of Jesus Christ who "made himself of no reputation (counted himself as nothing) and took upon him the form of a servant (slave)" and "humbled himself, and became obedient unto death, even the death of the cross." The "Obedient One" as

46. Thornwell, "Relation to the Church on Slavery," 383. Referenced in Tishby, *Color of Compromise*, 85.

47. Thornwell, "Relation to the Church on Slavery," 381; Tishby, *Color of Compro-mise*, 85.

48. Thornwell, "Rights and Duties," 49–50.

the "servant-of-servants" was one with whom the enslaved could identify and find solace in their suffering. This portrayal of Jesus Christ offered the enslaved a passive paradigm of one who by virtue of his patient suffering was worthy of their emulation in daily relationships with their "masters" and with one another. It was made clear to them that Jesus "chose" to be an exemplary "servant-of-servants" and many masters would favor those who consented to be Christlike in their servile status over those who "chose" to remain unconverted. The goal of this christological paradigm was to promote a model of humble, suffering, and obedient Christlike comportment among the enslaved that would mold their will to the will of their earthly "master" in the name of Jesus Christ or "as unto the Lord." In the second development of this christological model, the enslaved would be taught to recognize that, not only was Jesus Christ as a *doulos* the savior of their souls, but Jesus Christ in his exaltation as *kyrios* ("lord") should be recognized as the "Compassionate Heavenly Slave/Master" who has entrusted their bodies to the stewardship of their earthly "masters" who serve on his behalf.

The Christ hymn of Phil 2:5–11 proved useful to the proslavery mission to establish a racialized Christian slavery. In the first place, Jesus Christ's salvific role as an obedient slave (*doulos*) up to his crucifixion, could be readily exploited by Protestant missionaries and preachers as a model for the slave's obedience to their earthly masters. Secondly, in the same manner, the salvific role of Jesus Christ who after his crucifixion/sacrifice was exalted as lord (*kyrios*) because of that same demonstration of slave-like obedience, served well as a model for slaveowners who because of their "sacrifices" to bring the gospel and religious instruction to the enslaved, are exalted to the most important position in history—stewardship (lordship) over enslaved blacks. They are the chosen race who have brought salvation to those who would have remained lost without their benevolent intervention. The result of racialized Christian slavery was that the white, earthly planters perceived themselves as elevated to a highly exalted place over enslaved blacks, who must bow, serve, and pay due homage to them "as unto the (heavenly) lord." For this reason, the in-Christ identity of white Evangelical (proslavery) Christianity posed a danger to African Americans and their quest for social justice. The life and experience of Josiah Henson can be read as a cautionary example of an African American who had benightedly inculcated too deeply the in-Christ identity promoted by white Evangelicalism.

The Danger of Appropriating White Evangelical "in-Christ Identity"

The narratives of Josiah Henson, a formerly enslaved preacher who escaped slavery in 1830 from Port Tobacco, Maryland and became an abolitionist and founder of a black settlement in Canada, is quite interesting. He recounts his life and conversion in several different writings.[49] Henson had a dramatic conversion experience at the age of eighteen and relates the impact upon him of hearing for the first time about the love and cross of Jesus Christ.[50] When Henson heard the message of the gospel, he was caught up in the rapture of recognizing his humanity and self-worth— "He [Jesus] loves me," he exclaimed, "He died to save my soul." This was not something he had heard before and caused him to ponder his life of enslavement. "In sharp contrast with the experience of the contempt and brutality of my earthly master," he remarks, "I basked in the sunshine of the benignity of this divine being. He'll be my dear refuge—he'll wipe away all tears from my eyes." His conversion experience gave him the strength, he recalls, to bear things that seemed difficult before, and he now felt sorry that "'Massa Riley' didn't know him [Jesus], sorry he should live such a coarse, wicked, cruel life." Nevertheless, "[s]wallowed up in the beauty of the divine love, I loved my enemies, and prayed for them that did despitefully use and entreat me."[51] Henson, before his encounter with the message of the gospel and the knowledge that Jesus loved him and died for him and for all humankind, felt that he had *no human value*, that he was considered nothing more than a brute animal fit for unrelenting toil. This was the goal of proslavery ideology: to remove or eliminate any sense of human value and personal worth in the souls of black folks to exploit their physical labor. But in hearing the message of the cross of Christ, Henson's journey toward wholeness and human dignity began and eventually his life would be transformed, and he would preach the gospel himself. In his desire to fulfill his duty as a Christian to his "earthly master" as a trusted Christian and overseer, and now also to Jesus Christ as his "heavenly master," his inculcation of proslavery "Christ-like" deportment would in due course cause him to commit what he called his "unpardonable sin."

49. Henson, *Narrative*, Henson, *Truth Stranger than Fiction*, 27–30; and Henson, *Father Henson's Story*.

50. Henson, *Narrative*, 11–13; Henson, *Life of Josiah Henson*, 27–28; Henson, *Autobiography of the Rev. Josiah Henson ("Uncle Tom")*, 30.

51. Henson, *Autobiography*, 32.

Henson acknowledged that he had a passion for freedom but confessed that he had never dreamed of running away.[52] It seems that his long tutelage in the proslavery Christian ethics of enslavement, fostering his humble and submissive Christ-like posture, would have tragic consequences for himself, his own family, and his enslaved companions. It happened that in 1825, Henson's "master" entrusted him with the responsibility of transporting a large number of his enslaved companions, including his wife and children, from Maryland to Kentucky. His "master" having become financially strapped, asked his most trusted overseer, Josiah Henson, to lead all his other enslaved persons to his brother's farm in Kentucky, where they would be free from his creditors' claims. As a faithful Christian and trusted overseer, Henson approached his duty seriously as one who had imbibed deeply the in-Christ identity promoted by Evangelical preachers, remarking regretfully after gaining his freedom: "The duties of the slave to his master as appointed over him in the Lord, I had ever heard urged by ministers and religious men." On their journey by boat up the Ohio River, and passing along the Ohio shore, Henson and his companions "were repeatedly told by persons conversing with them that [they] were no longer slaves but free men, if [they] chose to be so." Henson relates further that: "At Cincinnati crowds of coloured people gathered round us, and insisted on our remaining with them. They told us we were fools to think of going on and surrendering ourselves up to a new owner; that now we could be our own masters, and put ourselves out of all reach of pursuit." However, because of his sense of Christian duty and religious pride, Henson said that he "sternly assumed [the role of] the captain, and ordered the boat to be pushed off into the stream." He would lead the entire group back into slavery! Only after it was too late, did Henson comprehend the cost of his loyalty to the proslavery slave-code of ethics. He declared that: "Often since that day has my soul been pierced with bitter anguish at the thought of having been thus instrumental in consigning to the infernal bondage of slavery so many of my fellow-beings." Henson would eventually rebel, flee to Canada, and live to regret his "unpardonable sin" but would become an abolitionist advocating for the end of slavery in effort to redeem his youthful mistake. It was certainly Henson's inculcation of the "Christ-like" comportment of proslavery Christology—of the humble, dutiful, and faithful portrayal of Jesus Christ, which was promoted especially for enslaved

52. Quotes and references on Henson's discussion of is "unpardonable sin" are from Henson, *Autobiography of the Rev. Josiah Henson ("Uncle Tom")*, 42–48.

blacks, who was "*obedient* [as enslavers expected all the enslaved to be] unto death"—that caused him to miss the golden opportunity of freedom for himself, his family, and his enslaved companions.

Henson declared that: "I had a sentiment of honour on the subject [that is, to be obedient to his earthly master and to do his "God-given duty" as a Christian, despite his enslavement]. The duties of the slave to his master as appointed over him in the Lord, I had ever heard urged by ministers and religious men." Once he gained freedom, however, he understood the impact of proslavery ideology upon his self-image as a Christian: "I have wrestled with God in prayer for forgiveness. Having experienced myself the sweetness of liberty, and knowing too well the after-misery of a number of these slaves, my infatuation [with his Christ-like duty] has often seemed to me to have been the unpardonable sin. But I console myself with the thought that I acted according to my best light, though the light that was in me was darkness. Those were my days of ignorance. I knew not then the glory of free manhood, or that the title-deed of the slave-owner is robbery and outrage."[53] Henson's greatest life's regret was that he had inculcated too much of proslavery preaching and Christology to recognize their manipulative effects on his life and that of his enslaved companions, which made him willingly deny himself and others the freedom they deserved. Yet, it was his acceptance of the pro-slavery in-Christ identity that garnered the attention of one who would become Antebellum slavery's most potent enemy and who also wielded a most powerful weapon—the pen of Harriet Beecher Stowe.

Harriet Beecher Stowe's compelling abolitionist novel *Uncle Tom's Cabin: or, Life Among the Lowly* was published in 1852. Josiah Henson's first published narrative *The Life of Josiah Henson, Formerly a Slave, Now an Inhabitant of Canada, as Narrated by Himself* appeared in 1849, eight years after he had escaped to Canada, and his book caught the attention of Stowe. She had been thinking for some time about how she might address the subject of slavery, especially in its relation to Christian churches and Christianity and thought seriously about producing a book that "would show the wickedness and horrors of the slave-trade, and thus promote its overthrow."[54] Accordingly, Stowe, after reading Henson's narrative, requested a meeting with him to which he agreed and provided for her

53. Henson, *Autobiography of the Rev. Josiah Henson*, 47–48.

54. John Lobb [editorial note] in Henson, *Autobiography of the Rev. Josiah Henson*, 10.

further details about his life when he was enslaved. Thus, from his book and personal interview (and interviews with a few other individuals familiar with Southern slavery), Stowe derived the primary material for *Uncle Tom's Cabin*. John Lobb who edited and wrote an editorial note for the book on Henson's life, *The Autobiography of Rev. Josiah Henson ("Uncle Tom")* written in 1881, offered a glowing review of Stowe's masterpiece of antislavery literature while also confirming that Henson was the real "Uncle Tom" (a badge of honor Henson proudly wore and promoted on his speaking tours). Lobb says,

> . . . that remarkable work of fiction, the circulation of which has been exceeded by that of no book save the Bible, and which our author may be forgiven for believing was 'the wedge that finally rent asunder' the gigantic fabric of American slavery 'with a fearful crash.' Yet such, in spite of the nursery protest that 'Uncle Tom' was killed in the book, and that Father Henson, therefore, can be no more than his ghost, is an undoubted fact, as a glance at the chapter on her hero in Mrs. Stowe's 'Key to Uncle Tom's Cabin' must convince any reader.[55]

Lobb confirms once-and-for-all for incredulous readers that Henson is the real-life inspiration behind the compelling character of Uncle Tom. Stowe used Henson's experience wherein he had fully inculcated proslavery Christology, which understood the social role of enslaved blacks through Phil 2:7–8 (in accordance with the suffering, humiliated, obedient Christ). But she differs from proslavery Christology in her understanding of Christ's exaltation (Phil 2:9–11) in which proslavery preaching assumed that whites were already experiencing God's favor as the (exalted) superior race. To the contrary, slavery did not exalt the white race, she argued, but demeaned it because the white race did not hold allegiance to Jesus Christ and the cross, blacks did: whites' allegiance is to Rome and its values—aggression and dominance. Stowe insightfully inverted the ideas of many missionaries and preachers who had spent years trying to convince Southern planters that Christianity made blacks better slaves. She reasoned that since blacks' "natural docility" made them the best slaves, they also made the best Christians, and domineering whites because of their temperament made them the worst Christians. "In order to become better Christians," she argues, "White people must constrain their domineering temperament

---

55. Henson, *Autobiography of the Rev. Josiah Henson*, 14.

65

and the evil outgrowth of that temperament: slavery."[56] With this clever twist of proslavery ideology/Christology, Stowe wrote her novel and created a "Christ-like," "cross-bearing" slave character that would change the views of many white Americans on the institution of slavery (but not on black inferiority!), and aiding in her cause was the life experience of Josiah Henson, the real "Uncle Tom." While Henson's conversion experience did not immediately compel him to seek his physical freedom, but on the contrary, white Evangelical preaching and teaching of a skewed in-Christ Christology helped to deepen his sense of proslavery Christian duty to his earthly enslaver. Appropriating their in-Christ identity for himself resulted in his denial of freedom and justice for himself and others. It was only later that he recognized the danger of appropriating white Evangelical in-Christ identity—which amounts to the religiously justified denial of justice and equity for black peoples! I suggest that contemporary white Evangelicals are seeking to promote a newly conceived in-Christ identity (but with the same results) to deny black people the justice they deserve and for which they have been fighting for centuries.

Conclusion

White supremacy having been conceived and nurtured by the modern concept of race has corrupted in-Christ identity by exalting "whiteness" as the core of Christian identity. The elevation of one group's ethno-racial identity as the foundation or basis of in-Christ identity was something that Paul fought against vehemently among the early communities of Jesus-followers. Christian identity has been so coopted by whiteness that many think that this identity is universal and unassociated with empire and its prerogatives. Whites have rarely had to consider whether their white identity (race or "whiteness") was more important than their Christian identity. Why? Because they have never seen the two as separate! Whiteness is not a color or racialized in the minds of many. Whiteness is universal, colorless, above and beyond racial categorization. White Evangelical Christianity taking up the mantle of white supremacy emphatically emphasized the "saving black

56. Kendi, *Stamped from the Beginning*, 193–94. Kendi observes further that for Stowe: "Blacks being more feminine, 'docile, Child-like and affectionate,' . . . allows Christianity to find a 'more congenial atmosphere' in Black bodies . . . . Blacks were spiritually superior because of their intellectual inferiority . . . This spiritual superiority allowed Blacks to have soul" (194).

souls" but not empowering black lives! It was designed to define, delimit, and determine black life, so that is would not interfere with or significantly disrupt white society and its privileges. In slavery, segregation, and beyond, white Evangelical Christianity has viewed enriched and empowered black lives as a threat to white society, its security and social stability. Black Christians of all denominational commitments must reevaluate the basis of their in-Christ identity shaped by whiteness. The real challenge of the Christ hymn and Paul's example is for Christians to deny those ethnic markers and privileges that would cause one group to exalt themselves over another. The example of Christ is marked by a willingness to deny one's status and privilege for the purpose of joining in partnership with those who have suffered historic injustices in society (in the hymn, that was slaves) and taking up their cause. This is the challenge of the Christ hymn, in my estimation, for white Evangelical Christianity.

5

Mainstreaming the Minoritized

Galatians 3:28 as Ethnic Construction

SZE-KAR WAN

THE STRIKING DECLARATION IN Galatians 3:28, "There is no Jew or Greek, no slave or free, no male and female, for all of you are one in Christ Jesus,"[1] continues to trouble professional exegetes and lay readers alike.[2] This grand vision—one that has been called "revolutionary,"[3] a "new form of human community,"[4] a "Magna Carta of Humanity"[5]—is also fraught with problems. Foremost among them is a tyranny of oneness. It opens itself up to the possibility of cultivating an oppressive conformity that could threaten the elimination of all forms of diversity and differences. There is disagreement on its meaning, interpretation, significance, or impact, to be sure, but what remains most jarring is how calls for radical equality and inclusivity exist side by side with coercive conformity and compliance.

This problem manifested itself during the Reformation already and continues to exert influence on the West today. In his 1535 *Commentary on Galatians,* Martin Luther interpreted this verse as a call for unity but

---

1. Unless stated otherwise, I am responsible for all translations of the biblical text.

2. As can be imagined, relevant literature on Gal 3:28 is vast. See discussion by Keener in his 2019 commentary, *Galatians,* 297–319.

3. Bruce, *Galatians,* 191.

4. Wright, *Galatians,* 244.

5. Witherington, "Rite and Rights," 593, attributing the phrase to Krister Stendahl.

added that such unity could be accomplished only by outlawing differences and crushing dissents:

> . . . in Christ there is *no law, no difference of persons*; there is neither Jew nor Grecian, but all are one; for there is but *one body, one spirit, one hope of vocation*; there is but *one gospel* . . . . Here, therefore, the conscience knows *nothing of the law*, but has *Christ only* before her eyes . . . . if [Christ] be taken out of our sight, then comes anguish and terror.[6]

"No difference of person" is ostensibly a response to inequality mentioned earlier but sounds ominous like an interpretation of the line "there is neither Jew nor Greek." Indeed, Luther's commentary takes a sinister turn with two statements rejecting the "law." The law is contrasted to Christ: "In Christ there is no law." The law must be replaced by Christ: "The conscience knows nothing of the law, but has Christ only before her eyes." While "law" is frequently used in the commentary as a cipher against works righteousness of the Catholic Church, Luther often lumps "Papists" together with "Jews and Turks" as those who reject his "Christian" doctrine of justification.[7] In his discussion of the law as παιδαγωγός, which he translates as "schoolmaster" (3:24–25), Luther attacks the Jews for loving and obeying their Moses.[8] While commenting on πάντες γὰρ υἱοὶ θεοῦ ἐστε διὰ τῆς πίστεως ἐν Χριστῷ Ἰησοῦ (3:26), Luther makes an explicit rejection of the Torah: "He saith not, ye are the children of God because ye are circumcised, because ye have heard the law, and have done the works thereof, (*as the Jews do imagine, and the false apostles teach,*) but by faith in Jesus Christ."[9] So framed, the unity called for in his interpretation of Gal 3:28 with the stress on oneness ("one body, one spirit, one hope of vocation") can only mean a *Christian* unity based on the "one gospel," and it can be achieved only by abolishing all things non-Christian, which is to say, Jewish.[10] In so doing, Luther effectively shortens the phrase "there is no Jew or Greek" to "there is no Jew"! Under these restrictions, Luther's conclusion that "If [Christ] be taken out of our sight, then comes anguish and terror" must be read

---

6. Luther, *Galatians,* 429–30; emphasis supplied.

7. Luther, *Galatians,* 136, 151, 152, 230, 249, 465–67, 528, etc.

8. Luther, *Galatians,* 420.

9. Luther, *Galatians,* 426; emphasis supplied.

10. Luther explicitly says: "Now it shall be enough that we have shewed, that Paul speaketh not here [Gal 2:16] of the ceremonial law only, but of the whole law"; Luther, *Galatians,* 236.

not so much as a description of what might happen without Christ but as a *prescription for* "anguish and terror"—violence, in other words—against anyone found outside the Christian orbits. In Gal 3:28, therefore, Luther managed to gather all ingredients necessary for a Christian triumphalism that trained its tools of violence on the Other, in particular the Jewish Other—all in the name of oneness.

Those immediately affected were Jews. In the judgment of biographer Martin Brecht, Luther's antisemitism was fueled by an interpretation of the Bible:

> [Luther] regarded the Jewish religion and its adherents in a nega-
> tive way and wished that they would convert to Christianity . . . .
> His opposition to the Jews . . . was in its nucleus of a *religious and
> theological nature that had to do with belief in Christ and justifica-
> tion,* and it was associated with the understanding of the people
> of God and *the interpretation of the Old Testament.* Economic and
> social motives played only a subordinate role.[11]

As events even within Luther's lifetime show, his antisemitism had real-world bloody consequences when he openly called for violence against the Jews because of their refusal to convert to Christianity.[12] Centuries later, his writings and actions would directly inspire the Nazis. As one of his first acts when installed as head of the pro-Nazi Protestant Conference, Ludwig Müller raised the Swastika at the Wittenberg All Saints' Church where Luther had nailed his ninety-five theses, thus publicly and officially integrating Luther's Reformation into Nazi ideology. One can draw a straight line from Luther's exegesis to Nazi violence against the Jews.

This tyranny of oneness casts its long shadow on modern times as well. Ernest Burton, former president of the University of Chicago and the one-time chair of the American Baptist Foreign Mission Society who had been deeply involved in missionary efforts to China, in his highly influential

11. Brecht, *Luther,* 350; emphasis supplied.

12. The quote above from Luther's commentary on Gal 3:28 is preceded by: "In the world, and according to the flesh, there is a great difference and inequality of persons, and the same must be diligently observed. For if the woman would be the man, if the son would be the father, the servant would be the master, the subject would be the magistrate, there should be nothing else but a confusion of all estates and of all things"; Luther, *Galatians,* 429. In other words, Luther was perfectly content with keeping the social status quo while ignoring the social implications of the second antinomy of Gal 3:28, "there is no slave or free." What "equality" there is—if his antisemitism could be called that—must be confined to only the "spiritual" sphere, even though it eventually resulted in physical violence.

1921 Galatians commentary in the prestigious International Critical Commentary series, comments on Gal 3:28 as follows:

> The sweep of [Paul's] thought carries him beyond the strict limits of the question at issue in Galatia to affirm that all distinctions are abolished, and to present an inspiring picture of *the world under one universal religion* . . . . It is *only* in the religion of Christ that Paul conceives that men can thus be brought together.[13]

In subsuming the broad statement "all distinctions are abolished" under the imperialistic "one universal religion" with no apology, Burton leaves no doubt that the sameness he calls for is achievable only through Christianity. He does not make it explicit but simply assumes this "universal religion" to be Protestant, White, and male. That this is the case is clear from his insistence that the eradication of distinctions can be understood only "from the point of view of religion." In other words, Burton denies the grand vision of Gal 3:28 carries any social implications in the real world. He insists on one notable exception, however: the "indirect social significance" of erasing differences between Jews and gentiles, with "indirect" referring to the eventual triumph of Christianity and the demise of Judaism.[14] Paul's words demand no social or gender equality in real life, according to Burton, only a religious parity of sorts. With respect to ethnic differences, all must be subsumed under a universalism defined by White male Protestantism.

If White male Protestantism is the only "one universal religion" capable of promoting peace and equality, no other religion or belief system can be, least of all Judaism. If only White males can bring about universal peace, then women and other racial minorities are incapable of it and should never be put in a position to do so. In Burton's exegesis, a call for inclusivity and equality is made to promote exclusion and chauvinism. At a time of authoritarianism and rising nationalism around the globe, at this critical moment when the Bible is weaponized for violence and coercion, it seems urgent that we confront head-on the destructive potentials of this biblical text and, if necessary, defang it.

---

13. Burton, *Galatians*, 206; Horrell, "Paul, Inclusion and Whiteness," 125–26. Horrell suggests that Burton's comment is related to America's rising global economic dominance and his involvement in the China mission.

14. Burton, *Galatians*, 206–7. See also Horrell, "Paul, Inclusion and Whiteness," 126. The rest of Horrell's article is devoted to a history of interpretation on Gal 3:28 from the perspective of Whiteness.

Unbearable Tensions

A starting point is to note the intrinsic tensions that exist between Gal 3:28 and the rest of Paul's writings, even within Galatians itself. Thematically, only the first pair of opposites on ethnicity Jew/Greek is directly relevant to the ongoing discussion on whether adult male gentiles should be circumcised.[15] Paul otherwise makes no use of the slave/free or the male/female antinomies in Galatians.[16] Regarding the second antinomy, "there is no slave or free." Paul nowhere attempts to address inequality between slave and free or to question, let alone reform, the institution of slavery in Roman society. Whatever might have been his intentions or personal limitations, he does insist on sending the run-away slave Onesimus back to his master Philemon, thus restoring the social status quo of his days.[17] He advises slaves not to seek manumission but to be content with being a "freedperson who *belongs to the Lord*" (1 Cor 7:22), safely relegating freedom to the spiritual realm while ignoring the social reality associated with the inhumanity of slavery. "Let each remain *with God* in whatever state in which one was called" (1 Cor 7:24), he counsels, thus neutering any impetus for reforming or transforming the institution of slavery. Whatever social stations believers might find themselves to be in, Paul asks them to look for freedom only in the eschaton. When the parousia was delayed to an indeterminate future, the eschatological was ineluctably transformed into an empty promise, forever deferred but never realized. When we judge his corpus as a whole, therefore, there is ample justification to accuse Paul of allegorizing the physical into the ethereal and spiritual while leaving social ills intact, no matter how dehumanizing they are or however much they contradict the egalitarian visions of the Jesus-movement.[18] This can be documented even within Galatians itself. Paul's rhetoric builds on, in fact assumes, an unbridgeable gulf between slave and free in his allegory of Sarah and Hagar. He compares "the

15. Martyn, *Galatians*, 380.

16. I am not persuaded by Keener's suggestion that all three antinomies are deliberately introduced by Paul to anticipate the theme of inheritance (4:1—7); *Galatians*, 305). Paul's discussion of inheritance in 4:1—7 assumes an unbridgeable gulf between slave and son; it is far from a shining example of rectifying social differences.

17. Petersen, *Rediscovering Paul*, advances a sympathetic and defensible interpretation of Paul's position on slavery, taking into account of his principles and limitations. That, however, does not change the yawning gulf between the ideals enshrined in Gal 3:28 and the inability of Paul's and the early Christ assemblies to realize said ideals.

18. So Boyarin, *Radical Jew*, passim but especially 19–22.

present Jerusalem" to children of the slave woman Hagar, while calling the "free woman," the unnamed Sarah, "our mother" (4:25–26). The contrast between the earthly Jerusalem and the heavenly Jerusalem is understandable only within a context in which the distinction between slave and free is fundamental and unquestioned. The ironic use of freedom and slavery in his parenesis (5:13) assumes the same distinction.

The same tension also haunts the third antinomy of Gal 3:28, "There is no male and female." Paul's assemblies provided opportunities for women to exercise leadership, with Phoebe and Priska (Rom 16:1, 3) being prominent examples. But his letters in general and statements on women specifically betray no systematic attempt at addressing gender inequality or the power differential based thereof. The opposite is true, in fact. Paul's citation of a similar saying in 1 Cor 12:13 ("For in one spirit all of us were baptized into one body, *either Jews or Greeks, either slaves or free,* and all of us were made to drink of one spirit") includes only Jews/Greeks and slaves/free. The third pair male/female, which is explicitly cited in Gal 3:28, is omitted and might well have been replaced with a statement reinforcing rather than eliminating gender hierarchy (1 Cor 11:2–16).[19]

As is often noted, the form of the third pair of antinomy cited in Gal 3:28 is different from the other two: It reads "there is no male *and* female" as opposed to "no Jew *or* Greek, no slave *or* free." Its resemblance to the language of LXX Gen 1:27 ἄρσεν καὶ θῆλυ ἐποίησεν αὐτούς ("*male and female* he created them") is intentional and is likely the result of an allusion to a "myth of the primordial androgynous" before the differentiation of genders.[20] Such a view would fit in well with an apocalyptic pattern that looks forward to a future return to our pristine prelapsarian past when decay and death of the fallen creation give way to the "new creation" (6:15). That this is part of a broad *Endzeit-Urzeit* pattern found in many forms of apocalyptic Judaism should not be doubted. According to that pattern, the hopes and expectations of humanity will be realized at an end time envisioned as a return to the beginning of creation.[21] This primordial myth is represented

19. See below for a fuller discussion of 1 Cor 12:13 and its relationship to Gal 3:28. For now, suffice it to note most recognize that 1 Cor 12:13 is a paraphrase of the original Gal 3:28; MacDonald, *No Male and Female,* 6–7, 116–17. Macdonald is followed by virtually every scholar after him. The infamous "women be silent" passage (1 Cor 14:33b–36) is a later, non-Pauline gloss, in my judgment.

20. Meeks's conclusion ("Androgyne," 185) is followed by virtually every commentator after him. See the latest survey by Keener, *Galatians,* 308 and n880.

21. Stendahl, *Bible and Role of Women,* 32. Stendahl, however, identifies the new

by an androgynous figure who is pre-gendered and non-ethnic. Wayne Meeks calls it a "reunification myth," because it speaks to reuniting our long-lost opposite halves.[22] This androgynous myth has profound implications not just for "reversing" gender differentiation but also for the erasure of ethnic differences.

That Paul has inserted an existing formula into the present context to make his point seems certain, but judging by the tension the formula maintains with his thoughts at large, his arguments in Galatians in particular, it seems equally certain that the formula did not originate with him. Structurally, Gal 3:27–28 interrupts the thought that flows from verse 26 to verse 29, as can be seen in the following arrangement:

26: For all of you are children of God in Christ Jesus through faith;

27a: for as many as you were baptized into Christ

27b: have put on Christ.

28a: There is no Jew or Greek,

28b: there is no slave or free,

28c: there is no male and female,

28d: for all of you are one in Christ Jesus.

29a: If you belong to Christ,

29b: then you are Abraham's seed,

29c: heirs according to promise.

"Through faith" (v. 26) is likely added by Paul to connect this section to 3:23–25 where Paul claims a new epoch of faithfulness has been inaugurated to replace the law. Furthermore, since verse 26 is parallel to verse 28d, with "children of God in Christ Jesus" (v. 26) parallel to "one in Christ Jesus" (v. 28d), Paul is likely the author of those two lines as well. Verse 27a points to the occasion for the formula—namely, baptism—with "as many as you" being constructed to anticipate "all of you" (v. 28d). That leaves verses 27b–28c as the original form of the tradition:

27b: You have put on Christ,

28a: there is no Jew or Greek,

---

creation with the church. See also Keener, *Galatians*, 309. Betz, *Galatians*, 190: "The claim is made that very old and decisive ideals and hopes of the ancient world have come true in the Christian community." Also Martyn, *Galatians*, 380–83; see below for critique, however.

22. Meeks, "Androgyne," 180–81.

28b: there is no slave or free,

28c: there is no male and female[23]

The phrase "you have put on Christ" (Χριστὸν ἐνεδύσασθε), with the verb in the middle with an accusative personal object, appears nowhere else in the Pauline letters. Distant parallels are found in a discussion of the end time in 1 Cor 15:53–54, but there Paul uses the verb metaphorically to describe our natural body being replaced by a resurrected body: perishability "to put on (ἐνδύσασθαι) imperishability" and "mortality to put on immortality." Some have argued that the language here is Septuagintal.[24] But the parallels are inexact; examples adduced in support are closer to Paul's metaphorical usages. Others have tried to take the usage figuratively in the sense of "[taking] on the characteristics, virtues, and/ or intentions of the one referred to, and so [becoming] like that person."[25] But the absolute and pity tone of Gal 3.28 seems to indicate something deeper than emulating the moral exemplar of Christ. In sum, none of the examples advanced as parallels comes close to the idea of "putting on" and "putting off" a redeemer figure. The closest parallels are found in gnostic and proto-gnostic texts, as Hans Dieter Betz has long shown, where they appear also in the context of baptism.[26]

Baptism appears nowhere else in Galatians prior to the introduction of this primordial myth, and it plays no role in the subsequent discussion. That is a strong argument that the tradition was part of an early liturgy recited to and by initiates as they underwent baptism into the Jesus-assemblies.[27] Confirmation can be found in the similarly worded saying in 1 Cor 12:13 where the reference is also baptism: "For in one spirit all of us were *baptized* into one body, either Jews or Greeks, either slaves

23. MacDonald, *No Male and Female*, argues that a Dominical Saying reconstructed from the *Gospel of the Egyptians*, *2 Clement*, and the *Gospel of Thomas* lay the foundation for the Galatians formula; see especially 14–16, 113–32.

24. Das, *Galatians*, 382; and Keener, *Galatians*, 303–4.

25. Longenecker, *Galatians*, 156; Oepke, "δύω," 319–20. This baptismal context is accepted by virtually every scholar.

26. Betz, *Galatians*, 188–89 and 188n60–61. The origins of the myth underlying Gal 3:28 are too complex to be considered here, nor is the question central to my purpose here. For survey of options, see MacDonald, *No Male and Female*, 1–16.

27. Meeks, "Androgyne," 166 and passim. This is the majority opinion among scholars: See Betz, *Galatians*, 181–85; Longenecker, *Galatians*, 154–55; deSilva, *Galatians*, 336–37.

or free, and all of us were made to drink of one spirit."[28] Here the style
is prosaic instead of liturgical and the structure looks nothing like the
parallelism of the Galatian formula. As noted above, only two opposite
pairs, Jews/Greeks and slaves/free, are included; the third, male/female,
is missing. Moreover, the two opposite pairs mentioned in 1 Corinthians
are listed in the plural and are stated positively: *both* Jews *and* Greeks,
both slaves *and* free are included in the one body. These differences have
significant consequences. In 1 Corinthians Paul is attempting to integrate
disparate groups into the same organization through baptism without de-
nying their identities as Jews and gentiles or their social stations as slaves
and free. Dennis MacDonald suggests that "perhaps we should assume
that [in 1 Corinthians] he never intended to deny the existence of social
distinctions but that he intended to celebrate them in the acceptance of
all people in the new creation."[29] In Galatians, on the other hand, the
baptismal formula is used to question exclusion.

Three conclusions can be drawn from this comparison. First, if the
statement of 1 Cor 12:13 is related to the baptismal formula of Galatians,
as it seems certain, the latter more than likely represents the more original.
Other than the liturgical stylistic differences, it seems more reasonable to
assume Paul dropped the male/female pair in his letter to the Corinthians
given his issues with women leadership than the unlikely possibility that
he added it to a letter that makes no mention of it. The second conclusion follows the first: Paul's statement in 1 Corinthians is a paraphrastic
citation of the liturgical formula and therefore his own views towards
ethnicities and social classes. In Paul's mind, he is convinced that Jews
and Greeks, slaves and free can and should be integrated into one body—
reserving at best an ambivalence towards the eradication of gender differences. Third, if his statement in 1 Corinthians represents his personal
understanding of the baptismal formula, we must not assume facilely that
Paul completely agrees with the liturgical saying he cites from tradition.
The primordial androgynous myth denies all distinctions, be they ethnic,
social, or gendered, and it does not fit into the arguments in Galatians
without modification or reinterpretation. That is why Paul could not appropriate in for his discussion with the Corinthians until he recast it as

28. A similar formula also appears in the Deuteropauline Colossians in an implied
baptismal context, with language of "putting on" and "taking off" that recalls Paul's "putting on Christ" (Col 3:9–11), but it is unclear if the author of Colossians had borrowed
from and modified Galatians.

29. MacDonald, *No Male and Female*, 116–17.

inclusion.[30] In sum, Paul in Galatians cites verbatim a pre-Pauline—and judged by its tension with the rest of Paul's writings *non-Pauline* perhaps even *anti-Pauline*—baptismal formula to support his objection to circumcising adult male gentiles in the Galatian assemblies.

Primordial Androgyne

But what is the point of the original myth? How does Paul understand it and what purpose does it serve at this juncture in his argument? We can glean a clue or two from how male and female are understood in his letters. In 1 Cor 11:2–11 he explicitly uses the created order to reaffirm gender hierarchy and male priority: "For a man did not come out of a woman but a woman from a man, for a man was not created for sake of the woman but a woman for sake of a man" (1 Cor 11:8–9). This prompts Marie de Merode to dismiss Paul's use of Gal 3:28 altogether because of his inconsistent application:

> When we assess the enormous consequences attached to forbidding women from studying the Torah in Judaism, we can only be circumspect before wanting to maintain a decisive inequality and different treatment between men and women in the church. Paul realized attachment to circumcision would render true faith in Christ impossible. But did the maintenance of certain customs of Judaism, donning veil and above all silence and submission for women only, render true love, unity in Christ impossible?[31]

Merode's statement betrays a common but misguided tendency to blame Judaism for everything unsavory (in this case misogyny) while consigning all things honorable and good (true faith and true love) to the church. In spite of its shortcomings, however, her work points up, quite inadvertently, the distance between the myth encoded in the primordial androgyne and Paul's own practice. The grand vision of Gal 3:28 might have proved too radical for Paul. While Gal 3:28 represents an idealized, eschatological vision of the new creation, Paul attempts to modulate it by grounding it in Israel's covenantal context.

30. For a helpful discussion of possible authors of the baptismal formula and Paul's redaction, see MacDonald, *No Male and Female*, 5–14.

31. Merode, "Une théologie primitive," 189; my translation. See Kahl's defense of Paul's inclusion of the male/female theme, which might be prompted by a crisis in masculinity because of circumcision; Kahl, "No Longer Male."

Daniel Boyarin's observation in this connection is apposite but for one flaw. He writes: "For *Paul* male-and-female means neither male nor female in the non-corporeal body of the risen Christ. The individual body itself is replaced by its allegorical referent, the body of Christ of which all the baptized are part."[32] What Boyarin attributes to Paul belongs properly to the framer of the original baptismal liturgy, which Paul resists as well. The non-gendered androgynous figure represents a denial of the flesh and blood, the generational, the undifferentiated. But because gender is also tied to ethnicity, both being marked by and located in the body, the primordial androgynous figure in its purest form denies cultural and ethnic specificities as well. Both gender and ethnic diversities were devalued by the myth. Boyarin juxtaposes these two starkly:

> Flesh is the penis and physical kinship; it is the site of sexuality, wherein lies the origin of sin; it is also the site of genealogy, wherein lies the ethnocentrism of Judaism as Paul encountered it. All of these could be opposed, Paul came to see, by a spiritual or ideal set of counterparts which would enable the escape from the two elements of human life that Paul felt most disturbing: desire and ethnicity.[33]

The escape from "desire and ethnicity," again, should be attributed not to Paul but to the disembodied, spiritual vision encoded in the androgynous myth. For all of Paul's flaws of ethnocentricity and misogyny, devaluing the bodily is not one of them.

Louis Martyn likewise mistakes the myth for Paul's own positions. He observes that there is an inherent tension between Paul's "old-creational" and "new-creational" thinking. This is especially clear in places where he relies on the created order to make his case, such as when he accuses gentiles for their unwillingness to know God in Rom 1:18–32.[34] That is certainly true with his reaffirmation of gender hierarchy in 1 Cor 11:8–9, as we have seen. According to Martyn, Paul in Galatians relies on the baptismal formula to pivot to a new-creational perspective, and that helps him overcome differences in gender and ethnicity:

> Thus, the corporate people is determined to no degree at all by the religious and ethnic factors that characterized the old creation

32. Boyarin, *Radical Jew*, 24; emphasis supplied.

33. Boyarin, *Radical Jew*, 68. See also his critique of Robinson, *Body*, 21–22, 25, on 281n20.

34. Martyn, *Galatians*, 381.

(5:6; 6:15). This people is determined solely by incorporation into the Christ in whom those factors have no real existence. The church, in short, is a family made up of *former Jews and former gentiles*, not an enlarged version of a family that already exists.[35]

The church is thereby interpreted as the new family that transforms "former Jews and former gentiles" into a new collective consistent with the new creation, a new *ethnos* that goes beyond old divisions replacing them with a new *Christian* identity. Martyn comes to this conclusion no doubt because he senses an irreconcilable tension between old and new creation, but he is very much mistaken in identifying the church as the realization of a new people. As I have argued elsewhere, nowhere does Paul designate the church as the New Israel or even a new people, as if it constituted a "third race" as understood by second-century patristic writers.[36] It is highly doubtful that Paul had formulated a full-fledged ecclesiology in the manner of Colossians and Ephesians.

What most scholars fail to appreciate is that not only did Paul find a return to a pre-gendered state as suggested by the androgynous myth too radical for his taste, but he might have also found a resolution of the other two antinomies equally unpalatable. In his conception, the eschatological vision to be disclosed in the new creation must remain in the future. A premature realization before its time, by artificial means no less, would spell the end of Israel. As he explains in Romans, God's promise to Israel is irrevocable (Rom 11:29; cf., 11:1–2), and the world will be saved *only through* the salvation of Israel: ἄχρι οὗ τὸ πλήρωμα τῶν ἐθνῶν εἰσέλθῃ καὶ οὕτως πᾶς Ἰσραὴλ σωθήσεται, "until the time when the fullness of gentiles comes in and *in that manner* all Israel will be saved" (11:25–26). The future passive σωθήσεται ("will be saved") points to the end time when Israel is reserved as the only avenue through which the new creation is to be realized, and οὕτως refers to the manner in which the said eschatological vision is being realized, that is, the incorporation of gentiles. According to Paul's apocalyptic schema, the gentiles play an integral part in the end time, when the "fullness" of their conversion is attained, before "all Israel will be saved."[37] But before the end time comes, gentiles are to come in as

---

35. Martyn, *Galatians*, 380–83 (quote from 382); emphasis supplied.

36. Wan, *Romans*, 23–24. On Paul and the third race, see Buell, *Why This New Race?*

37. According to Jeremias, "Römer 11:25–36," ἄχρι οὗ indicates purpose and εἰσέλθῃ refers to the conversion of gentiles. I am less persuaded, however, by the proposal that πλήρωμα refers to "the predestined number of the elect according to an apocalyptic

gentiles, not as Jews; they will be incorporated into Eschatological Israel only when the new creation is fully realized.[38] Gentiles will be saved, in other words, "to be rescued from the coming wrath" (1 Thess 1:10), only as a part of Eschatological Israel—not independently and most definitely not as a separate *ethnos*.

Against this apocalyptic backdrop, Paul's designation of the baptized as "Abraham's seed" immediately after his citation of the baptismal formula does not look so incidental: "If you belong to Christ, then you are Abraham's seed, heirs according to promise" (Gal 3:29). However Paul might have understood the primordial androgynous myth, the only way it is acceptable to him is if it is to be realized in conjunction with Eschatological Israel. "No Jew or Greek" is acceptable to Paul only if it is interpreted as referring to "Abraham's seed" in the sense developed in Galatians 3. Paul's argument begins in 3:6–9, where LXX Gen 15:6 is used to show that Abraham was reckoned righteous as a result of having trusted God (Gal 3:6). He then combines LXX Gen 12:3 and 18:18 to come up with a conflated reading, "All the gentiles will be blessed in you" (Gal 3:8). The proof is a terminological one, as E. P. Sanders has shown long ago: "Abraham is . . . the middle term, being connected with gentiles in one proof-text and righteousness by faith in another."[39] Paul thereby asserts at the outset the means by which gentiles receive the Abrahamic blessings is to trust, in God presumably, "alongside faithful Abraham" (σὺν τῷ πιστῷ ᾿Αβραάμ, 3:9), i.e., emulating the example of Abraham.

By the time the argument progresses to the end of the first subsection, Paul demonstrates to the Galatians that they have already received the promise originally made to Abraham. The proof is in their reception of the eschatological Spirit: " . . . , in order that (ἵνα) the blessing of Abraham might come upon the gentiles in Christ Jesus, in order that (ἵνα) we might receive the promise of the Spirit through faith" (3:14). "Promise of the Spirit" should be taken as apposite, meaning "the promise which is the Spirit" or, better, "the promised Spirit."[40] In tying the Galatians' reception and experiences of the Spirit, which Paul mentions three times in

---

scheme" (Jewett, *Romans,* 700), hence my translation here simply as "fullness," leaving its meaning ambiguous.

38. For elaboration of this point, see Wan, *Romans,* 48–52, where I use "Ideal Israel" for Eschatological Israel.

39. Sanders, *Paul, Law, Jewish People,* 21.

40. See Wan, "Promise of the Spirit," 211n7.

the opening verses of this chapter (3:2, 3, 5), to the promises God made to Abraham as part of the covenant, Paul seeks to prove to the Galatians that, by dint of their observable experience of the eschatological Spirit, they have indeed been blessed with the promises hitherto available only to Abraham and his descendants.[41]

Paul's argument reaches its zenith in 3:29 when he claims that gentiles—because "they belong to Christ"—are now considered the "seed of Abraham" (3:29). As Caroline Johnson Hodge has recently shown, "seed of Abraham" had a long history going back to Ezra of being deployed "to draw a firm and permanent boundary around Israel," even though others allow for incorporating outsiders into the fold.[42] Paul's creative exegesis of the Abrahamic passages clearly shows an openness to including gentiles in the covenant.[43] He grants gentiles entrance into the covenant of his forbears, even though in the allegory of the olive tree in Rom 11:17–24 he also makes a distinction between the original occupants of the covenant and latecomers.[44] In Galatians, for purpose of dissuading adult males from going through with circumcision, it is enough for him to convince them that at baptism, which they underwent "in faith" and at which point they have "put on" Christ, they have already been incorporated into the covenant. Christ is Abraham's only "seed" (3:16) and gentiles are now adopted as Abraham's seed because they have put on Christ at baptism.[45] Inasmuch as Peter and those who align with him Judaize (2:14), Paul himself also Judaizes. He is as engaged as Peter is in persuading gentiles to live the Jewish

41. For details of argument, see Wan, "Promise of the Spirit."

42. Johnson Hodge, "Question of Identity," 159–64; quote from 161. See 161n25 for the permeability of ethnic boundaries.

43. I am not completely persuaded by Johnson Hodge ("Question of Identity," 164 and passim) and Fredriksen (*Paul,* passim but especially 158) that in Paul's conception gentiles remain gentiles even after incorporation. Their arguments are subtle and multifaceted, but they and I might differ on our understanding of parameters of ethnicity and *ethnos.* Suffice to say, my thesis here does not depend on whether it is legitimate to call the in-Christ gentiles "Jews" or "Judeans." For my purpose, it is enough simply to note that Paul is successful in grounding the primordial androgynous myth in the establishment of the Jewish *ethnos.*

44. The reason has to do with keeping self-important *gentile* converts from overtaking the Roman assembly. His purpose in Galatians is different. Here he is more concerned with stressing the *inclusion* of gentiles in the fold.

45. For baptism as adoption, see Betz, 187; Johnson Hodge, "Identity," 162; Johnson Hodge, *If Sons,* 67–116.

way.[46] They differ only on the means by which gentiles become members of the covenant. While his detractors insist on circumcision as a sine-qua-non condition for entrance, Paul counters that it is Jesus Christ's faithfulness (πίστις) that makes it possible for gentiles now to trust God in the same way Abraham did.[47] "The debate was not between a static, rigid form of Jewish ethnocentrism and a supposedly more flexible, more inclusive form of universalism. Rather, both narratives were attempts at restructuring Judaism to accommodate the entrance of gentiles."[48]

Conclusion

What implications does the foregoing examination of Gal 3:28 have for race relations today? First and foremost, we need to remember that ethnicity is never fixed or immutable. Every culture and every ethnic group maintains boundaries of some form, without which there can be no group cohesion or integrity. These boundaries serve to distinguish insiders from outsiders—so long as in-group members agree on where these boundaries are, what characteristics are to be considered essential, what common experience should define said group, what origin myths should in-group members subscribe to, and so on. But none of these criteria is ever considered immutable; even bloodline was open to modification during the Roman period through adoption. That is the basis for Paul's willingness to grant gentiles the status of Abraham's seed. Whatever ethnic markers are used to mark insiders from outsiders, they represent a composite snapshot of what in-group members consider crucial for the ongoing life of a group *at that moment* and where they agree to draw their ethnic boundaries for the time being. By common consent, conscious choice, environmental factors, or external events, sometimes gradual sometimes sudden, an ethnic group could decide to move its boundaries for purpose of including hitherto outsiders deemed valuable to the life of the group or, conversely, exclude members deemed harmful. The Greek term *ethnos* from which our term "ethnicity" was derived was after all malleable and applicable to a wide range of people groups.[49]

46. For discussion of the notion of Judaization, see Cohen, *Beginning*, 179–97; Fredriksen, *Paul*, 112.

47. Wan, "Galatians," 250–52.

48. Wan, "Galatians," 258.

49. I have explored this topic in relation to the Asian American experience in a number of publications: see, e.g., Wan, "Diaspora Identity"; Wan, "'To the Jew First'"; and Wan, "'Body of Christ.'"

My study of Galatians confirms this view in broad outline. It bears repeating that the issue that gives rise to Galatians is not a debate between Christianity and Judaism; to study the letter thus is to perpetuate an anachronism that has yielded deadly fruits. Instead, we encounter two competing constructions of the Jewish *ethnos*. Paul argues against advocates who insist on a stricter separation between those born Jewish and those born gentiles unless the latter keep kosher food requirements and undergo circumcision, rituals Paul derisively calls "works of the law" (2:16; 3:2, 5, 10). They consider these steps necessary to become full converts and therefore full members of the Jewish *ethnos*. In opposition, Paul insists that all who "belong to Christ" must be considered legitimate members already; there is no need for additional requirements. In a clever rhetorical argument, Paul suggests that making additional demands is tantamount to making Christ a "deacon of sin" (2:17) because it would be a silent acknowledgment that Christ is not sufficient in himself. In his crowning argument, Paul uses a liturgy used on the occasion of their baptism *qua* adoption that looks forward to the final consumption of the new creation (3:28), but he hastens to add a correction grounding the apocalyptic vision of the baptismal formula in the flesh-and-blood experience of Physical Israel and the Jewish people by explicitly calling the Galatians "seed of Abraham" (3:29).[50]

This seems like an unsatisfactory solution for Western interpreters who have been conditioned for half a millennium since the Reformation to privilege the oneness of Gal 3:28 over Paul's corrective in the following verse. The baptismal formula, ostensibly at the verbal level, demands flattening rather than promoting differences. That was never an issue in the Imperial and Colonial West until recent decades and then only among the so-called "progressive" interpreters who preferred to understand the erasure of differences as the basis for liberation, empowerment, equality, and so on[51]—even though the verse could just as well be read, for example

50. The obvious question, why Paul rejected kashrut and circumcision for adult male gentile believers, is too complex to be considered here because of time and space. But suffice to say that they were rejected *not* because for their supposed ethnocentricity, since both Paul and his detractors advocated for the Jewish *ethnos* and were engaged in ethnic construction. Other than its historical difficulties, this typical position of the so-called New Perspective on Paul reintroduces an anti-Jewish interpretation that has plagued Protestant theology ever since the Reformation.

51. Braxton, *No Longer Slaves*, 95, credits the verse for addressing racial equality. The interpretation of Gal 3:28 as liberation and empowerment has a rich history among African Americans, as Lisa Bowens has richly documented in her book *African American Readings of Paul*. For example, Julia Foote uses it to overcome prejudice

by the likes of Martin Luther and Ernest Burton, as promoting a Christian hegemony.[52] The formula by itself, wrested from its argumentative context in Galatians, is pithy and cryptic; it is an ideological Rorschach giving interpreters free rein to work out whatever they wish for with little exegetical basis or justification. A recent commentary on Galatians is a case in point. The author argues that the purpose of the baptismal formula, attributed to Paul, is:

> to preserve social diversity rather than to eliminate it. It is Paul's opponents who are seeking to eliminate diversity. They want gentiles to adopt circumcision, to Judaize, to become Jews, losing their distinction in identity. Paul wants unity between gentiles as gentiles and Jews as Jews, all together in Christ . . . ."[53]

While this is an admirable position I wholeheartedly support, the commentary provides no exegetical path that leads from "no Jew or Greek . . . , for we all are one in Christ" to "unity between gentiles as gentiles and Jews as Jews." Since we do not observe the dissolution of ethnic (understood as fixed) or gender differences after baptism, so goes the argument, that could not have been Paul's meaning.[54] So Paul's opposition to circumcision is taken to mean that he does not want to make gentiles into Jews, even though as we have seen above Paul has no trouble calling them Abraham's seed in the next breath. The same criticism could be leveled against my own of Gal 3:28 as the eradication of "power differentials."[55] While I still hold to that understanding as an ethical desideratum, it was a conclusion reached without exegetical justification. The reason for this lacuna seems clear to me now. The oneness of the original baptismal formula was

against her as a woman (172, 185), and William Seymour thinks it calls for racial unity (215), which was later revived by Charles Harrison Mason into an "all-inclusive egalitarian fellowship" (223).

52. See, e.g., critiques of Paul's preservation even promotion of hierarchy in general, which is at odds with the supposed egalitarianism of Gal 3:28 by Castelli, *Imitating Paul*; and Marchal, "Queer Approaches."

53. Oakes, *Galatians*, 128. Oakes's is more of an ethical than an exegetical solution: " . . . what does it mean to say 'There is no Jew nor Greek'? . . . Eliminating social distinction, without eliminating diversity, means practices such as eating together showing love and forbearance to one another, bearing one another's burdens, and not engaging in division, envy, or devouring one another" (128).

54. Oakes, *Galatians*, 129: "The point of the paradoxical assertion of the nonexistence of evidently continuing social polarities is that being in Christ brings oneness, unity, across these polarities."

55. Wan, "Diaspora Identity," 126.

to be achieved by the erasure of ethnic, social, and gender differences, but the nature of these differences was never specified. Paul co-opts it to serve his ethnic construction by interpreting oneness in Christ to mean being incorporated into the promise as Abraham's seed—without, it must be said, clarifying *what* is being eliminated.[56]

Can Paul be accused of promoting ethnocentrism? Even racism? Let us not forget that his thought, life, experience, indeed his world, centered around his ethnic identity as an apocalyptic Jew, and in the etymological sense he was surely ethnocentric. But if that is the case, calling outsiders Abraham's seed turns out to be the highest honor Paul could bestow gentiles. It is no accident that Abraham is so central to this argument.[57] As the first convert, Abraham provides a paradigmatic path—through *pistis*—for gentile believers to negotiate through the ethnic boundaries; as the father of the Jews, he grants—through his seed Christ—insider status to those who have been baptized and adopted into him. For Paul, Abraham was a universal figure accessible to all. As he delineates in Romans, Abraham can be the father of both the uncircumcised and the circumcised (Rom 4:11–12), which is his way of saying Jews and Greeks or the totality of humanity (Rom 1:16; 2:9–10; 3:9; 10:12). The promise made to Abraham, which to Paul is being fulfilled as gentiles are brought into the fold, is that he would inherit the world (Rom 4:13). No mere tribal ethnarch, Abraham is destined to inherit the whole *kosmos* and become the father of all humanity. That anyone else other than Abraham could be the father of all humanity would not even be a rejected possibility to Paul. Taking the patriarch of an ethnic group to be the progenitor of all human beings is, by definition, ethnocentric.

We should therefore refrain from expecting Paul to act like a modern liberal guided by principles of equality and non-judgment. For when he tries to deal with the thorny relationship between Jews and gentiles, as he does in Romans, solutions he offered are invariably issued from his Jewish toolbox and, just as invariably, they prioritize Jews over gentiles (Rom 11:17–24). There is ample reason why his writings, not to mention those by his second and third-generation followers, have been used to underpin

56. Paul does not in Galatians say if gentiles will remain gentiles and Jews will remain Jews or, if they remain distinct, specify the power relationship between them. In the allegory of the olive tree, however, he does distinguish gentiles from and subordinate them to Jews (Rom 11:17–24).

57. Whether Abraham was first brought up by Paul or by his opponents makes no difference.

racism, misogyny, ethnonationalism, Christian nationalism, and all forms of hegemonic ideologies and regimes.

To make Paul's ethnocentricity a basis for the ideology of domination, however, would be a grave misreading of Paul. To return to the second half of our question, whether Paul can be thought of as a racist, the answer is an unequivocal No. Racism is fueled by a power differential. It subscribes to a system of domination that ascribes goodness, competence, independence, and privilege, to one race or ethnicity while ascribing wickedness, incompetence, dependence, and shame to another. To one race is the power given; to another power is denied. Paul's apocalyptic Judaism operates from a position of weakness within the imperial context. When he proclaims that "all Israel will be saved" (Rom 11:26), he looks forward to the rescue of an oppressed minority whose daily survival is perpetually in doubt. He takes his position of weakness as a given but all the while looks forward to a redemption that can only be described as otherworldly instead of insurrectionist (Rom 11:26–27). His ethnocentricity is as far from systemic racism as can be.

Properly read, Paul is no friend of hegemons, tyrants, fascists, and supremacists. Nevertheless, that has not stopped them from enlisting Paul for purpose of domination. Indeed, it is particularly ironic, and nefarious, that fascist and supremacist groups have become so skilled at co-opting Paul by claiming victimhood. From the Nazis who used a supposed need for *Lebensraum* to justify invasion and annexation to modern American White Christian nationalists who claim to be in danger of being "replaced" by NonWhites, they all rely on some twisted form of grievance, manufactured or real, to access Paul. That is when Paul's ethnocentricity becomes most dangerous, but that is the space where we need to be most vigilant.

PART III

Paul, Empire, and Community

6

The Pursuit of Impossible Hospitality

Reading Paul's *Philoxenia* with Jacques Derrida

Jeehei Park

Introduction

I AM PART OF a voluntary diaspora in the United States. I chose to move
from South Korea to the United States as a young adult and to become a
naturalized US citizen. I have spent my adult life mostly in the northeastern
region of the States and now in Austin, Texas. I have held many immigration statuses—from an international student to a resident alien and then to
a naturalized citizen, and each process and set of paperwork was onerous
and pricey. Yet regardless of my status, I have been seen and treated as a
perpetual foreigner. Through the repeated and relentless experience of living as the "other" in this white-centric American Empire, where I belong
remains elusive and inconsistent. What "home" means to me has become
more entangled as what "home" needs to be like has become less and less
clearly defined. Recently, when I returned to the US from overseas, I was
surprised when the TSA agent greeted me with "Welcome home!"

Such ambivalence around what home signifies and how it is defined
is hardly novel. The conventional concept of "home" is often and aptly contested. Avtar Brah's words are penetrating when she says,

> Where is home? On the one hand, "home" is a mythic place of
> desire in the diasporic imagination. In this sense it is a place of no
> return, even if it is possible to visit the geographical territory that

is seen as the place of "origin." On the other hand, home is also the lived experience of a locality.[1]

This essay participates in this discourse of diaspora in which home is constructed and fluid. In it, I wish to navigate a more complex dimension of the politics of home by calling particular attention to hospitality, the praxis of welcoming others. There is no need to reiterate how much harm against newcomers, immigrants, and their descendants has sprung from the unchecked and unchallenged attachment to "home." Engaging hospitality to challenge the prescribed notions of home and belonging might sound ironic. What prompts me to do so is, most simply, the repeated invitation from a host to a guest to "Make yourself at home." For whenever I am invited to make myself at home, I wonder: Does the person saying it mean it? Are they really inviting me to make their home mine? By extension, when a country ostensibly offers such hospitality to foreigners, whether asylum seekers, visa holders, or refugees, does the country, and its people, really welcome them to the extent of letting them blur the border or take down the wall—literal or metaphorical—that separates their homeland from mine? More fundamentally, do we really welcome *all* foreigners?

The spirit and practice of welcoming strangers are often considered the most Christian or biblical response to immigration. This essay examines Paul's words in Rom 12:13 where he explicitly speaks of hospitality. He employs the Greek word *philoxenia*, which is a compound word composed of *philos* and *xenos*, literally meaning "love of the stranger." Coupled with his message on unity, Christians in general pick this verse to highlight and mandate hospitality as a practice that leads to cultural and racial/ethnic diversity and inclusion. They present hospitality as a good deed, strategize it as a set of "how-tos," and in doing so, easily gloss over its complexity and extensiveness.

To make my argument, in this first part of this essay, I show that some interpretations of Rom 12:13b have narrowed down the scope of hospitality by marking it as an act needed in specific situations or as a strategy of evangelism. I then introduce and engage Jacques Derrida's deconstructive approach as a theoretical trajectory to demonstrate that hospitality, which seems to efface the divide between "us" and "them," ironically often thickens and deepens it instead. For Derrida, hospitality is impossible to achieve, yet should nonetheless be pursued. Considering

1. Brah, *Cartographies of Diaspora*, 192. Homi K. Bhabha's notion of "unhomeliness" is also relevant. Bhabha, *Location of Culture*, 13–25.

Derrida's view, I position Paul's *philoxenia*, which is distinctive from and also disruptive of imperial hospitality, as a core element of his gospel, one that is conducive to the life of the *ekklēsia*.

Paul's *Euangelion* in Rom 12–15

A brief inquiry into the context of 12:13 within Romans helps map out the rhetorical aim of *philoxenia* vis-à-vis the gospel that Paul is preaching to the Romans. Verse 12:13 is located in the last section of this letter, 12:1—15:3, which is categorized as paraenesis, commonly understood as a moral exhortation.[2] Paul's tone changes markedly in 12:1; he begins the section by saying, "Therefore I exhort you." Commentators have aptly observed the exhortatory character of this section; Martin Luther wrote regarding the opening of ch. 12, "The apostle is about to teach a Christian ethic," and Victor Furnish noted that thirty-one of the forty-two imperatives in this letter are found in Rom 12—15, a sudden clustering.[3]

Scholarly attempts to shed light on the nature and purpose of this paraenesis center on two questions. The first one has to do with the section's relationship with the preceding chapters in this letter: Is this paraenesis as an appendix to the theological treatise found in chs. 1–11? Most topics in chs. 12—15, such as the church as one body and the reconciliation between the strong and the weak, are often considered subsidiary to Paul's messages on justification by faith and the salvation of Jews, which appear in chs. 1—11.[4] Many exegetical writings and commentaries deal disproportionately with chs. 12–15 since ethical instructions are viewed as less substantial for being less theological. Karl Barth, for example, lumps chs. 12–15 into a single chapter of his commentary after spending a chapter on each of chs. 1—11.

The second question revolves around the breadth of Paul's teaching. Is he trying to teach a general ethic or to respond to circumstances peculiar to the Roman community? The more traditional stance on this question is that Paul's ethical teaching in chs. 12—15 is a general "exposition

---

2. Malherbe, *Moral Exhortation*, 124-25. For more updated views on paraenesis, especially in Paul's letters, see Popkes, "Paraenesis in the New Testament"; Engberg-Pederson, "Concept of Paraenesis"; Aasgaard, " 'Brotherly Advice.' "

3. Furnish, *Theology and Ethics in Paul*, 99.

4. One exception would be 13:1-7.

of obedience" corresponding to the dogmatic teaching in chs. 1—11.[5] By contrast, Jeremy Moiser argues that the discord between Jewish believers and gentile believers is the situation in chs. 12—15, and thus, Paul's instructions in this paraenesis section aim for the reconciliation between the groups.[6] Ernst Käsemann offers a middle way. He argues that 12:1—13:4 is Paul's general exhortation and that 14:1—15:13 is his more specific message targeted at problems in the Roman *ekklēsia*.[7]

Paul's own situation, which is the context that Paul himself explicitly identifies in this letter, is, I think, key to grasping the purpose and scope of his exhortation in Rom 12—15. Paul wrote and sent this epistle to the believers in Rome prior to his impending arrival in Rome. In the letter, he seeks support from the Roman church (15:24), which he had not founded, on his way to Spain (1:10).[8] Thus, his primary goal is to convince the Roman believers of his *euangelion* so they will accept him as an apostle and support his mission work.

What, then, is Paul's *euangelion*? The core of his good news is that salvation is now also available to "everyone who has faith, to the Jew first and also to the Greek" (1:16). Paul presents himself as a "minister of Christ Jesus to the gentiles, in priestly service to the *euangelion* of God, in order that the offering of the gentiles might become acceptable" (15:16). Throughout the letter Paul expounds on the racially/ethnically inclusive dynamic of salvation, which is his response to the Jew-gentile relationship vis-à-vis *pistis tou christou*.[9] Jews, without abandoning the law, and gentiles, without following the law, are parts of God's promise, and both, as they are, are equal constituents of the *ekklēsia*.

Paul's *euangelion* response to the question as to the Jew-gentile relationship is concerned with racial/ethnic inclusivity, and this illumines two characteristics of his paraenesis in Rom 12—15. This exhortation section is a practical thread of his gospel, not an afterthought following a theological treatise, as Frank Matera argues: "The goal of Rom 12:1—15:13 is not to lay down the foundation for ethics but to show the intimate relationship

---

5. Barrett, *Romans*, 212.

6. Moiser, "Rethinking Romans 12–15," 575.

7. Käsemann, *Romans*, 323.

8. According to Robert Jewett, Romans can best be characterized as a "letter of recommendation" written on his own behalf—in Koester's terms—or as a letter of "missionary diplomacy." Jewett, "Romans as an Ambassadorial Letter," 19.

9. For a recent summary of the discussion on *pistis tou christou*, see Easter, "Pistis Christou Debate," 33–47.

between the gospel and life."[10] Paul attends to *how* his *euangelion* can oper-
ate in the *ekklēsia* and strengthen it. This practical nature of the *euangelion*
leads to the second feature of the paraenesis in Rom 12—15, namely that
Paul's exhortation is not a set of instructions on how an individual leads
an ethical life. Helmut Koester remarks, "Ethical conduct is not designed
to further one's own moral perfection, but to promote the welfare of the
neighbor and to build up the congregation."[11] Whether or not there was
actually tension between Jewish believers and gentiles believers in Rome,
Paul's situation demanded that he offer his gospel in such a way as to assure
the Romans that they, though coming from and with different backgrounds
and experiences, can build up the *ekklēsia* together. Rom 12—15 is a critical
component of Paul's *euangelion*, through which he hopes to convince the
Roman believers that his *euangelion*, by advancing practical and communal
ways for embrace and inclusion, will help the community grow together.
Paul's admonition for hospitality also needs to be understood as a component of the *euangelion* that accompanies the community's growth.

Exhorting Hospitality in Rom 12:13

I analyze some exegetical, theological, and homiletic understandings of
hospitality in 12:13b and identify some common thrusts found in them,
which I will interrogate in the next section. In Rom 12:13, Paul gives two
specific ethical instructions: to share in the needs of the saints and to pursue hospitality to strangers (*philoxenia*).[12] These two exhortations conclude
his teaching on what makes *agapē* genuine, which began in verse 9. Both
are fittingly presented as practices that make love genuine. Presumably,
he intended the Romans to read his call to participate in charity for the
"saints" in verse 13b alongside Rom 15:22—32, particularly 15:26, where
Paul speaks of the believers in Macedonia and Achaia who "made a certain
contribution for the poor among the saints in Jerusalem." Many commentators have construed 12:13a as being Paul's encouragement for the Roman
believers to extend their love toward Christ believers in Jerusalem, in other
words, to reach out beyond their own community.[13]

---

10. Matera, *Romans*, 284.

11. Koester, *Introduction to the New Testament*, 2:139–40.

12. All Greek translations are mine unless noted otherwise.

13. Johnson, *Reading Romans*, 184; Thiselton, *Discovering Romans*, 225.

Hospitality in 12:13b is understood in a similar fashion; it is another ethical action that believers are called to take as a demonstration of their faith. A notable number of commentaries, mostly written from historical-critical, literary, or theological perspectives, situate this practice of inviting and welcoming in the context of travel, which they commonly view as an integral part of the Christian mission in Paul's day. Widely found in commentaries is such historical contextualization of hospitality, and this is the first common thread I call out. Brendan Byrne argues that Paul calls the practice of hospitality a regular service because "many believers were constantly on the move, either for business or on a mission, or perhaps as a result of persecution and expulsion."[14] Douglas Moo makes a similar claim that the need for hospitality was urgent due to the many traveling missionaries and Christians.[15] Exegetes such as Käsemann and Arland J. Hultgren highlight how taxing and risky travel was in antiquity to situate the need for hospitality. According to Käsemann, itinerant apostles had to rely on the hospitable acts of Christians because "[G]ood lodgings were hard to come by in antiquity, especially in the capital and ports."[16] Hultgren marks hospitality as a practice through which that Christians could provide comfort and security to traveling missionaries who were exposed to various perils on the road. He comments,

> Since travel and staying at inns were both difficult and dangerous, hospitality within Christian homes was important for reasons of safety . . . Hospitality for travelers made Christian mission possible in the ancient cities of the world; without it, travel would have been so much more difficult and perilous.[17]

As such, hospitality is understood as a morally good act because it protects the vulnerable who travel—especially, here, those traveling for the sake of the good news—by welcoming and accepting them. Edward L. Smither, whose work centers on missiology and Christian history, evaluates hospitality as a pillar mechanism that enabled mission in the early church. He writes, "As the early Christian community expanded, Paul and other traveling evangelists routinely relied upon the hospitality of churches and Christian households to host them during their missionary travels."[18]

14. Byrne, *Romans*, 377.

15. Moo, *Epistle to the Romans*, 798.

16. Käsemann, *Romans*, 346–47.

17. Hultgren, *Romans*, 456. See also Dunn, *Romans 9–16*, 744.

18. Smither, *Mission as Hospitality*, 31.

Locating Paul's admonition for hospitality in the context of ancient travel gives rise to the second common thread of interpretation: the recipients of such hospitality are considered to be Christians. Hultgren furthers his interpretation with the argument that Christ believers in Rome "were especially in a position to offer hospitality to other Christians coming there."[19] David Lynn Bartlett makes it clear that Paul emphasizes the task of welcoming other Christians as the "job" of Christians in Rome because he hopes to visit there soon too.[20] It is highly likely that, as many of these interpreters have indicated, Paul and other traveling missionaries depended on the hospitality of the communities and their members throughout their journeys. Paul himself asks Philemon in 1:22 to prepare a room for him. Yet is welcoming fellow believers an act of hospitality or an extension of fellowship? Is *philoxenia* in particular oriented toward those who put themselves on the road to proclaim the good news? It boils down to the question of who is defined as *xenos*.

Commentators like Ben Witherington III and Robert Jewett posit the alleged conflict between Jewish believers and gentile believers as the immediate reason for this exhortation to show hospitality. According to Witherington III, Paul is asking the Romans to be hospitable toward "fellow Christians" as a way to bring reconciliation to the fragmented Roman church.[21] Jewett brings to the fore the possible situation that Jewish believers, who had left Rome due to the Edict of Claudius, were beginning to return to the city. On 12:13b Jewett writes,

> Although cast in general terms, consistent with the demonstrative rhetoric of Romans, some specific implications for the Roman church situation are plain. With a large number of Jewish Christian and other leaders returning to Rome after the lapse of the Edict of Claudius, evoking conflicts and hostilities, there was a concrete need for the kind of hospitality that marked the Jesus movement and subsequent Christianity.[22]

For Jewett, hospitality is a morally good act for gentile believers to show toward Jewish believers; gentile believers are obliged to accept and welcome Jewish believers back to the community. Both Witherington III and Jewett consider *philoxenia* in 12:13b to refer to hospitality toward Christians, either

19. Hultgren, *Romans*, 456.

20. Bartlett, *Romans*, 114.

21. Witherington, *Romans*, 294.

22. Jewett, *Romans*, 765.

known or unknown to the community. Whether hospitality is positioned either in the circumstances of mission and travel or in the situation of a Jew-gentile conflict, the beneficiary of hospitality is limited to Christ believers. Hospitality can certainly solidify intra-group relationships and forge cordial dynamics among the members. Nevertheless, is this the goal of hospitality in 12:13b? What is noteworthy is that Paul intentionally uses *philoxenia* here, which the NRSV translates as "hospitality to strangers" due to *xenos*.[23] Is hospitality then intended toward traveling missionaries or returning Jewish believers, and are they the strangers who need love? The question is again with regard to who *xenos* is with regard to the practice of *philoxenia*, to which I will turn in the following section.

The last interpretive propensity that I find quite common concerns the relationship between hospitality and evangelism. It is evident in Paul's admonition that the new life in the gospel entails many changes in terms of the believer's way of living, and the practice of hospitality is one of them. Ian Hussey takes Paul's message of *philoxenia* in Rom 12:13b as a biblical reference that shows that "Evangelism practiced in the context of hospitality is not simply the sharing of the knowledge of the gospel, but a demonstration of redeemed lives, transformed and sustained by the grace of God."[24] For Hussey, hospitality is evangelistic—not necessarily evangelical—because living in accordance with the gospel is conducive to practicing hospitality. For some, hospitality is also evangelical because welcoming and inviting people to dinner is an effective means of evangelism. Not surprisingly, this perspective is more usually advanced by evangelical preachers or writers. One excerpt from John Piper's sermon is representative. He preaches,

> So the command in Romans 12:13 is that hospitality not just be a once a year thing at Thanksgiving or Christmas, but a constant attitude and practice. Our homes and apartments should stand constantly ready for strategic hospitality—a readiness to welcome people who don't ordinarily live there.[25]

In this sermon titled "Strategic Hospitality," Piper envisages hospitality as instrumental in proselytizing more people. Eugene Peterson's message is not too different. He says, "When we realize how integral acts

23. Interestingly, 12:3b is either completely missing or merely cited in Koenig, *New Testament Hospitality*; Jipp, *Saved by Faith and Hospitality*; Nadella, "Embrace, Ambivalence, and Theoxenia."

24. Hussey, "Theology of Church Engagement," 219.

25. Piper, "Strategic Hospitality," August 25, 1985.

of hospitality are in evangelism, maybe we will be more deliberate and intentional about it."[26]

Reading *Philoxenia* with Derrida

Above, I set out three common threads found in several exegetical and pastoral interpretations of *philoxenia* in Rom 12:13b. First, those interpretations locate Paul's call to hospitality in the context of early Christian mission and travel; second, they identify other Christ believers as the recipients of hospitality; and third, they present hospitality as an apparatus for evangelism. My critical response to them is the foundation on which I construct Paul's *philoxenia* as unconditional and radical hospitality, as a *euangelion* that challenges imperial power, and thus, as a Christian practice that disturbs the border between home and foreign lands. I draw upon Jacques Derrida's concept of deconstructive hospitality as my theoretical interlocutor,[27] and as it were, structure my exploration around two questions: Who is the host? And who is *xenos*?

Who Is the Host?

What I am inquiring about is not the intention or motivation of the host nor the qualifications of the host. My focus is on the effect that a hospitable act has on the relationship between the host and the stranger—the one whom the host welcomes as a guest. Derrida gives an imaginary anecdote to describe how such a hospitable act can legitimate and reinforce the autonomous power of the host. He says,

> The master of the house having no *more urgent* concern than that of letting his joy shine out over anyone who, of an evening, will come to eat at his table and rest under his roof from the fatigues of the road, anxiously *awaits* on the threshold of his house the

26. Peterson, *Christ Plays In Ten Thousand Places*, 216.

27. Derrida was born into a Jewish family in 1930 in Algeria, a French colony at that time, and hence a French citizen from a birth. His citizenship was revoked in 1942 when the Vichy government denaturalized Algerian Jews. This led him to be excluded from the French public school system. He migrated to Paris at the age of nineteen to study at Louis-le-Grand. David Carroll, who worked with Derrida for almost twenty years, writes in his in memoriam note that he "never forgot how it felt to be a victim of discrimination, deprived of basic civil rights, and treated as an unwanted foreigner in his own land; to realize, as he put it, that he was a citizen of no country at all." Carroll, "In Memoriam."

stranger he *will see* rising into view on the horizon like a liberator. And from as far away as he sees him coming, the master will hasten to call out to him: "Enter quickly, as I am afraid of my happiness."[28]

Derrida accentuates the proactiveness, or even aggressiveness, in the host's act of identifying a stranger ("he *will see*") that the host will welcome into their home. The host takes the initiative of hospitality for the host's own satisfaction, not for that of the stranger. Richard Kearney elaborates on Derrida's stance by bringing into the conversation the etymological analysis of *hostis* done by Émile Benveniste, to whose work Derrida also refers.[29] Kearney introduces Benveniste's examination of *hostis* and *hospes*, both of which are the roots of hospitality in the Indo-European tradition of western culture. Furthermore, Kearney finds *hospes* relevant to exposing the power of the host, saying,

> The terms *hospes* and *hospites* contain the root word *pet, potestas*—power. So the host served as a sort of guest-master who had the capacity and authority to welcome or refuse foreigners into his home . . . *host* is a double term at the root of both hospitality and hostility.[30]

Hospitality, regardless of the host's intent, may actually precipitate and intensify the imbalance of power between the host and the guest as the host has the sole authority of turning the stranger into the guest by accepting them into the home. In doing so, the absence of agency for the guest is justified. It is here that I see a possible pitfall of locating 12:13b in the context of travel; traveling missionaries are put into the position of having no agency as regards the practice of hospitality. By suggesting this, in no way do I claim that early Christians provided lodging and food to itinerant missionaries to exhibit their sovereignty. But I do note that such contextualization may constrict the intent and scope of hospitality, which is not only a moral imperative but also a way of living out the *euangelion* every day, recasting it as a type of patronage. When misused in the hostile sentiment of migration, hospitality may amplify the dynamic that the host actively exercises the power to choose and welcome the guest and the guest passively relies on the benevolence of the host. This understanding of hospitality only thickens the

28. Derrida, *Of Hospitality*, 129–31.

29. Derrida, *Of Hospitality*, 21.

30. Kearney, "Hospitality," 177–78.

line between the host and the guest, and hence, becomes another medium through which the guest is "other"ed.

Who Is *Xenos*?

Derrida's response to the question of who the *xenos* is, is the aspect that makes his understanding of hospitality complex and deconstructive. Referencing Benveniste, Derrida remarks that the foreigner (*hostis*) can be welcomed "as guest or as enemy."[31] Kearney offers a more thorough account of not only dual but also contrasting meanings of *hostis* as follows:

> [O]riginally the notion of *hostis* involved someone in an equal reciprocal relationship demanding trust, a laying down of one's weapons, a conversion of hostility into hospitality. It was only later, when interpersonal or intercommunal relations of trust were replaced by abstract relations between impersonal states, that *hostis* assumed the connotations of enemy. Henceforth, hospitality was intrinsically linked to the possibility of hostility and so became a drama of choice and decision.[32]

Just as a foreigner can be welcomed as a guest, so too can the same person be rejected as an enemy. The choice and decision belong solely to the host, and this adds to the power of the host. By what criterion does the host make the call? Derrida's answer sounds even more poignant:

> How can we distinguish between a guest and a parasite? In principle, the difference is straightforward, but for that you need a law; hospitality, reception, the welcome offered have to be submitted to a basic and limiting jurisdiction.[33]

---

31. Derrida, *Of Hospitality*, 45. See the pun intended by Origen in his homily on Lot and his daughters: "When the angels who were sent to destroy Sodom desired to expedite the task with which they were charged, they first had concern for their host (*hospitis*), Lot, that in consideration of his hospitality (*hospitalitatis*), they might deliver him from the destruction of the imminent fire. Hear these words, you who close your houses to strangers; hear these words, you who avoid a guest as an enemy (*qui hospiteni velut hostem vitatis*)." Origen, "Homily V," 112. Interestingly, Derrida also takes the story of Lot as a tantalizing example of radical, absolute hospitality. Derrida, *Of Hospitality*, 151–53.

32. Kearney, "Hospitality," 177.

33. Derrida, *Of Hospitality*, 59–61.

This law for hospitality allows the host to exercise sovereignty "by filtering, choosing, and thus by excluding and doing violence."[34] This is a moment at which a state is involved in controlling and monitoring what and where is meant by "home."[35] The law of hospitality, which now protects the authority of the host in selecting guests and deciding whom to grant asylum, is "paradoxical and corrupting" and thus makes hospitality conditional.[36]

What Derrida hopes to elicit is absolute hospitality, a hospitality that is unconditional in that it goes above and beyond what is required or expected juridically. The first step to defying such a law of hospitality is to welcome foreigners without asking any questions. The host, according to Derrida, should not ask the foreigner's name, where they come from, or what they want:

> Let us say yes *to who or what turns up*, before any determination, before any anticipation, before any *identification*, whether or not it has to do with a foreigner, an immigrant, an invited guest, or an unexpected visitor, whether or not the new arrival is the citizen of another country, a human, animal, or divine creature, a living or dead thing, male or female.[37]

In other words, hospitality becomes unconditional when the *xenos* is welcomed, regardless of origin, status, gender, or any other category of identification.

The terminal shift that Derrida attempts to make is to strike down the borderline or distinction between the host and the foreigner. There is always a chance that a host can become a foreigner, and a foreigner a host. Derrida recounts two Greek narratives to demonstrate metaphorically the permeability of the line between host and foreigner. The first one is a dialogue between Socrates and a foreigner, who is anonymous in the conversation. For this foreigner to speak freely of his foreign ideas, Plato writes, Socrates steps back and mostly remains silent or jumps in with a question.[38] Socrates plays the role that is considered to be more appropriate to that of a foreigner, while the foreigner leads the conversation and speaks as a host. The other comes from Sophocles's *Oedipus at Colonus*, in which Derrida shows how Oedipus, the foreigner to the people of Colonus,

34. Derrida, *Of Hospitality*, 55.
35. Derrida, *Of Hospitality*, 51.
36. Derrida, *Of Hospitality*, 55.
37. Emphasis original. Derrida, *Of Hospitality*, 77.
38. Derrida, *Of Hospitality*, 5–11.

addresses those residents as if they were foreigners.[39] Oedipus, the outlaw who committed incest and parricide, Antigone, his own daughter who guides her father along their journey, and the inhabitants of Colonus are all depicted as foreigners for different reasons. Who then is the *xenos* here? All of them, or none of them? It becomes evident that the line dividing the host and the foreigner is mutable, arbitrary, and fictitious; for Derrida, this is another—and the most fundamental—reason that welcoming the foreigner into the home should be unconditional. The host is not in a position to impose restrictions such as saying, "As my guest, you must agree to act within the limitations I establish."[40] Also, it is not hospitality if the host does it as a duty or expects reciprocity. Derrida emphasizes,

> For if I practice hospitality *"out of* duty" [and not only *"in con-forming with* duty"], this hospitality of paying up is no longer an absolute hospitality, it is no longer graciously offered beyond debt and economy, offered to the other, a hospitality invented for the singularity of the new arrival, of the unexpected visitor.[41]

Derrida's view calls into question most interpretations of 12:13b that posit other Christians as the beneficiaries of hospitality. If the welcome is limited to Christians, particularly itinerant preachers, is it hospitality? Can Christ believers journeying from other places be considered strangers or foreigners who cannot return hospitable love? What is noteworthy is that in Rom 12:10 Paul is already pointing to *philadelphia*, which denotes familial love, especially among siblings. Paul uses *philadelphia* in 1 Thess 4:9–10a to indicate the same kind of love, saying, "Now regarding *philadelphia*, you do not have the need to have anyone write to you, for you yourselves have been taught by God to love another, and indeed, you do love all the brothers and sisters throughout Macedonia." Their *philadelphia* is for all siblings in Christ throughout Macedonia as well as in Thessalonica. Thus, *philadelphia* signifies love toward Christians, whether they are your fellows in your *ekklēsia* or elsewhere. In Paul's exhortation in Rom 12:9–13, *philadelphia* and *philoxenia* alongside each other comprise genuine *agapē*. That being so, *xenos*, the object of *philoxenia*, indicates an outsider, a stranger, who may not belong to the community and who cannot reciprocate in offering love.

Derrida himself is aware that absolute hospitality is impossible. Hospitality may be so gracious and generous that it is no longer simply a matter of

39. Derrida, *Of Hospitality*, 35.

40. Westmoreland, "Interruptions," 2.

41. Derrida, *Of Hospitality*, 83.

acting in an ethically appropriate way but goes far beyond such behavior.[42] Hospitality is far more difficult and complex than simply saying, "Make yourself at home" to your guests. If we pay attention to Derrida, it becomes obvious that hospitality cannot and must not be easily reduced to a moral obligation as a consequence of the new life in the *euangelion* or as a means for evangelism. Hospitality is not supposed to be easy or perfectly completed. Kearney summarizes the impossibility of hospitality, saying:

> The ethos of hospitality is never guaranteed. It is always shadowed by its twin: hostility. In this sense, hosting others—aliens and foreigners, immigrants and refugees—is an ongoing task, never a fait accompli.[43]

Interestingly, Derrida's impossibility is ironic because there is hopefulness in it. It means carrying something out with persistence, not giving up or being defeated.[44] Hospitality is not an exception; it is work that is always ongoing yet never entirely accomplished.

I find Paul's call in 12:13b to be a Derridean impossibility; Paul asks the Romans to "pursue" (*diōkontes*) hospitality to strangers. This exhortation is distinctive in the NT; he is not simply reminding them to not neglect it (Heb 13:2) or to be hospitable (1 Tim 3:2; Titus 1:8; 1 Pet 4:9). As Moo says, "Paul does more than that; he urges us to 'pursue' it—to go [all] out."[45] *Diōkontes* imparts to *philoxenia* a sense of being proactive, of being "vigorous intentionally," as Jewett puts it. Believers are asked to seek out strangers and to practice hospitality toward them, not merely to await the arrival of anticipated and well-respected guests. Though this is rarely discussed in the scholarly literature, I contend that Paul intends the wordplay in 12:13–14.[46] In verse 14a, Paul writes, "Bless those who persecute (*diōkontas*) [you]." One verb used back to back here in verses

42. Derrida takes as an example the story of Lot in Genesis, who offers his own daughters to the Sodomites in order to protect his guests. His intention is not to condone sexual abuse for the sake of hospitality, but to emphasize the impossibility of hospitality. Derrida, *Of Hospitality*, 151–55.

43. Kearney, "Hospitality," 173.

44. It is in this sense that Derrida calls justice impossible too. For more on this topic, see Derrida, "Force of Law," 3–67.

45. Moo, *Romans*, 798.

46. The only one I could find was Sze-kar Wan. He remarks, "Paul uses the same verb *diōkein* here as he does in the last verse, thus consciously linking loving those who threaten us with hostility to the pursuit of hospitality towards strangers." Wan, *Romans*, 55.

13–14—both in participle form—is *diōkein*, which has the double meaning of "pursue" and "persecute." The reader (or hearer) of this letter in Greek would intuitively perceive that pursuing love for strangers can precipitate being maltreated literarily, and perhaps, practically as well. The pursuit of hospitality may lead the way to hostility; the sovereignty of the host, in Derrida's terms, is not always secured.

Philoxenia as Impossible Hospitality

Derrida's vision sheds light on Paul's *philoxenia* as unconditional and absolute hospitality in four regards. First, believers who practice *philoxenia* are not to expect any reward in return. Second, a stranger is welcomed regardless of their connections and without any provisos, and a host has no power to exercise this welcoming. Third, the effect of such hospitality is to dismantle the walls or barriers between the host and the guest, and between what is home and what is foreign. Fourth and last, *philoxenia* is unceasingly pursued because *and even though* this is not a task that can be ever completed. In this last section of the essay, I demonstrate *philoxenia* as an impulse to disturb the imperial power system—represented as the "law" in Derrida's discourse—a system that justifies and perpetuates the disparity between the host and the guest and condones injustices, especially in the context of migration.

Philoxenia in the Roman World

To the Romans in general, hospitality was not something novel, neither as a concept nor as a practice. The custom of hospitality (*ius hospitii*) was highly regarded and widely encouraged in the Roman cultural world; the Romans associated it with *pietas* before Christians did, and writers such as Cicero and Seneca described *hospitium* as something "sacred."[47] Paul's *philoxenia* was a radical vision of hospitality in the first-century imperial world, especially in comparison to two other types of hospitality: *proxenia* and *theoxenia*.

Proxenia is the Greek word that was most aptly interchangeable with the Latin *hospitium*. Yet, "the Romans tended to treat this kind of

---

47. Jewett, *Romans*, 765; Nicols, "Hospitality among the Romans," 424–25. Both Cicero and Seneca call hospitality as a "most sacred" (*sanctissimum*) thing. Cicero, *Against Verres* 2.2.110; Seneca, *Controversiae* 8.6.17.

relationship more formally and legally than did the Greeks."[48] John Nicols shows that any relationship of *proxenia* (whether public or private) was generally initiated by a formal invitation and physically documented on the *tessarae hospitales*, meaning the "tokens of guest-friendship."[49] On these tablets were recorded "at least the names of the *hospites*, their intention to formalize a relationship, and the intention that the relationship should continue to future generations."[50]

Theoxenia originates from the Greek mythology that Zeus visited people as a stranger. Unless they want to displease the gods, people are therefore urged to welcome strangers, each of which can potentially be a god in disguise, unless they want to displease any gods.[51] This hospitality is built on a strict rule of give and take. Raj Nadella's evaluation is accurate in that "the concept of theoxenia places emphasis on the moral obligation of the host to the guest, but it also highlights responsibilities and obligations of the guest to the host."[52]

Philoxenia is distinguished from these two kinds of hospitality. Most important of all is that *philoxenia* is initiated by *philos*, "love," not by an invitation. As Christine Pohl astutely reminds us, *philoxenia* is "closely connected to love" etymologically and practically.[53] Paul encourages believers to practice *philoxenia*, to welcome strangers without knowing who they are or where they come from, and without anticipating what they might offer in return. Thus, *philoxenia* does not rely on the "law" of hospitality by which the host chooses the guest and secures their "home." Rather, *proxenia* and *theoxenia* are conditional and paradoxical in Derrida's terms since they allow the host to select foreigners who are identified and able to reciprocate the hospitality. In his letter to the Romans, Paul is calling believers to resist this domineering, imperial way of providing care and instead pursue *philoxenia* to defy the kind of power that *proxenia* and *theoxenia* are likely to reinforce.

48. Nicols, "Hospitality," 424.
49. Nicols, "Hospitality," 424–26.
50. Nicols, "Hospitality," 427–29.
51. Nadella, "Embrace, Ambivalence, and Theoxenia," 173.
52. Nadella, "Embrace, Ambivalence, and Theoxenia," 174.
53. Pohl, *Making Room*, 31.

Philoxenia in America Today

Paul's *philoxenia*, when read alongside Derrida, becomes a discourse with which we can urge acceptance and kindness but also address injustices taking place around migration in the US today. The US immigration system is frankly imperial; it welcomes only those who meet the US's criteria and imposes its rules on them, and through such formalization and filtering the system is granted even more power. We were all shocked in June 2022 when fifty-three migrants were found dead in an abandoned tractor-trailer in San Antonio. We were all appalled at images of US Border Patrol agents on horseback chasing and grabbing Haitian migrants at the border. All such tragedies and atrocities are not simply accidents or individual wrongdoings. They are systemic and intentional. They continue to happen because the more people are approved to join this country, the more authority is conferred on the system. This asymmetry of power is the basis of the audacity by which a previous president of this country felt permissible to say, "Why do we want these people from all these s***hole countries here? We should have more people from places like Norway." US immigration is not a system to welcome foreigners as long as it is based on and perpetuates the false belief that the border, both literally and figuratively, safely divides "us" from "them," and consequently, as long as it condones violence to force that belief.

Paul's message of *philoxenia* inspires us to rethink migration today. Paul exhorts the Romans to pursue unconditional hospitality to strangers out of love, not based on a *tessara hospitalis*. After all, welcoming strangers does not require or establish a system to secure the distance between the host and the guest nor does it guarantee any reward or return. Taking foreigners into one's home is in itself an enactment of the *euangelion* because it is a practice of love that can put the host in a vulnerable position and lead to a blurring of the border or boundaries between host and guest, us and them. In so doing, hospitality becomes unconditional. Paul's *euangelion*, as his concern about the Jew-gentile relationship shows, is all about the new reality in Christ, in which different people are invited to love each other and live together. Understood this way, Paul teaches *philoxenia* in Rom 12:13b as a way of participating in the gospel more than as an obligation of the gospel. It may be impossible for us to achieve the ideal of *philoxenia* completely, but, as Derrida insists, we are called to pursue it with persistence.

Conclusion

This essay is an experimental reading of *philoxenia*, literally meaning "love of strangers/foreigners," in Rom 12:13b, a hapax legomenon in Paul's letters. I engaged Derrida's notion of deconstructive, absolute, and radical hospitality as the main interpretive framework to argue that Paul's *philoxenia* entails welcoming and accepting strangers unconditionally. Many commentaries and writings situate Paul's message of hospitality in the circumstances of ancient travel and early church mission, restricting our understanding of hospitality as oriented only towards fellow Christians. Homiletical interpretations tend to understand and promote hospitality as a means of evangelism, not as an end in itself. Derrida's notion helps us articulate hospitality as a discourse with more extensive implications than an instruction about a specific context and more complex than a mere strategy. I construed Paul's *philoxenia* as unconditional hospitality; the host has no power to select guests, and the guest needs no particular identification or association to be welcomed. Therefore, *philoxenia* is an act that disrupts the dominant system or normal expectations in the system. Just as Rom 12—15 is considered the ethical and practical dimension of Paul's *euangelion*, not an addendum, so his message of *philoxenia* is a component of the *euangelion* as it guides us to reflect critically on how we relate to others. "Make yourself at home" may yet be impossible for us to mean genuinely. Yet we can begin by welcoming those who are rarely welcomed.

7

From Alienation to Inclusion

Reading Romans 3:21–26 from a Diaspora Lens

EKAPUTRA TUPAMAHU

ONE DAY I MET with a student after class. We edged into the conversation by talking about some assignments for the class. And then she asked me if she could tell me something. I saw the tears beginning to flow from her eyes. She told me she was really struggling with the readings in class. She could not understand the readings on the synoptic problem, the performative nature of the gospel, etc. She felt like a stranger in the entire conversation; it is so foreign to her. However, she told me that the reading that week from Febbie Dickerson's womanist reading of the story of Tabitha/Dorcas in Acts 9:36–43 hit her quite differently.[1] She got excited about this reading because she felt connected to it. As a black woman, she could see herself and her story there.

This conversation with her was a wake-up call to me, first because students often cannot see their stories represented in the biblical studies readings, and second because it became clearer to me that the production of writing is always embedded in a particular social story. She could not understand the discussion or conversation on the synoptic problem (for instance) simply because it is not part of her story. It is a white man's story.

We need more books, articles, and essays in biblical studies that represent stories other than the story of the European men in the nineteenth century that has frankly dominated almost every conversation on the Bible

1. See Dickerson, "Acts 9:36–43," 296–312.

in the twentieth and twenty-first centuries. Take Rom 3:21–26 as a case in point. Paul states:

> But now, apart from law, the righteousness of God has been disclosed, and is attested by the law and the prophets, the righteousness of God through faith in Jesus Christ for all who believe. For there is no distinction, since all have sinned and fall short of the glory of God; they are now justified by his grace as a gift, through the redemption that is in Christ Jesus, whom God put forward as a sacrifice of atonement by his blood, effective through faith. He did this to show his righteousness, because in his divine forbearance he had passed over the sins previously committed; it was to prove at the present time that he himself is righteous and that he justifies the one who has faith in Jesus. (NRSV)

This text has been discussed mainly in a theological way. Pauline scholars often and unsurprisingly argue that this is a critical text for our understanding of the doctrine of atonement.[2] After all, the interpretation of Paul's letter to the Romans has been shaped by the Protestant Reformation. It is a European Protestant story. The exact meaning of Pauline verses such as δικαιοσύνη θεοῦ[3] or πίστις Χριστοῦ[4] in verse 22 becomes a site of lively debate among these theologically-minded European Protestant scholars.

In this essay, I would like to tell the story of Rom 3:21–26 from a different angle, as an argument that Paul made because he is a diaspora person. Now, to be fair, Paul's discussion is framed in theological terms and theological debate on this passage is not entirely inappropriate. However, many scholars have not highlighted the interconnectedness of the social and the theological. Theology is also sociology in some ways. Theology does not emerge *ex nihilo*, out of nothingness, in a vacuum. Rather, theology is rooted in social relations, social struggles, and social dynamics. This social perspective has been largely absent in many theological discussions on this passage Rom 3:21–26. So instead of repeating this theological discussion among biblical scholars here, I will bring Paul's

---

2. For instance, see Carson, "Atonement in Romans 3:21–26," 119–39; Ribbens, "Forensic-Retributive Justification in Romans 3:21–26," 548–67; Songer, "New Standing before God Romans 3:21–5:21," 415–24.

3. Hays, "Psalm 143 and the Logic of Romans 3," 107–15; Smith, "God's Righteousness, Christ's Faith/Fulness, and 'Justification by Faith Alone' (Romans 3:21–26)"; Reumann, "Gospel of the Righteousness of God," 432–52.

4. Johnson, "Rom 3:21–26 and the Faith of Jesus," 77–90.

experience as a diaspora person to this text and try to shed light on the social aspect of Pauline theology.

One's theology is constructed on the foundation of one's social location. This is true also of Paul's theology. Because it is constructed on the foundation of his social location, we can only properly understand his theology in light of his social *locus*. I will show in this essay that Paul understands everyone as sinful and everyone as redeemed only through Christ thanks to his diaspora consciousness marked both by negative experiences of alienation and rejection, and positive identification with others. In other words, Paul's theology is informed by his diaspora consciousness. I explore this thesis in two sections. In the first section, I discuss the framework I use to interpret Paul, that is, Paul as a diaspora person under the rule of the Roman Empire. In the second part, I attempt to read Paul's discussion in Rom 3 from the point of view of the diaspora experience. My aim is to show that Paul's big claim that everyone is guilty (3:9–20) and that everyone is justified through Christ (3:23–24) reflects Paul's negative and positive diaspora consciousness.

Diaspora as a Hermeneutical Framework

The diaspora theory is complex both because it engages multiple disciplinary studies and because it is grounded in the complexity of diaspora experiences. That is to say, the experiences of the Chinese diaspora might be different from those of the Jewish diaspora or Indian diaspora, or Filipino diaspora. But how do we define "diaspora"? What makes it different from "immigrants"? Attempting to separate diaspora from migration conceptually, a sociologist of diaspora, William Safran, offers six now widely discussed characteristics of diaspora. He says of the diaspora that:

> 1) They, or their ancestors, have been dispersed from a specific 'center' to two or more 'peripheral,' or foreign, regions; 2) they retain a collective memory, vision, or myth about their original homeland—its physical location, history, and achievements; 3) they believe that they are not—and perhaps cannot be—fully accepted by their host society and therefore feel partly alienated and insulated from it; 4) they regard their ancestral homeland as their true, ideal home and as a place to which they or their descendants would (or should) eventually return—when conditions are appropriate; 5) they believe that they should, collectively, be committed to the maintenance or restoration of their original homeland and

to its safety and prosperity; and 6) they continue to relate, person-
ally or vicariously, to that homeland in one way or another, and
their ethnocommunal consciousness and solidarity are importantly defined by the existence of such relationship.[5]

These criteria are mostly focused on the homeland. Criteria 2, 4, and 6
seem to be overlapped. As Robin Cohen, another noted scholar of diaspora
study, points out, "Although this aspect [homeland] is clearly of crucial importance, there is some degree of repetition of the argument." [6] Moreover,
these criteria are also mainly based on the study of the Jewish diaspora that
Safran describes as "the ideal type"—although he himself acknowledges
that no other groups meet all these criteria.

Unsurprisingly, other scholars have criticized this set of criteria.[7]
Among them, James Clifford is the most prominent. Clifford argues that
although on the one hand, Safran's effort to give a definition to diaspora
is commendable, on the other hand, his insistence on the "pure" forms
of diaspora (those communities that meet his six criteria) is not helpful
at all, noting that "even the 'pure' forms are ambivalent, even embattled,
over basic features."[8]

Instead of "locating essential features," Clifford argues that paying our
attention to "diaspora's borders" might be more helpful.[9] What he means
by *borders* is "what it defines itself against."[10] That is to say, instead of giving positive content to what diaspora is, one needs to see what diaspora is
against, what it defines itself against, and what are its others. In the analysis
of modern diaspora communities, Clifford argues, "Diaspora are caught
up with and defined against: (1) the norms of nation-states and (2) indigenous, and especially autochthonous, claims by 'tribal' peoples."[11] What he
is proposing is that if we want to analyze what diaspora is, we need to examine diasporic people's entanglement with the norms of the nation-state
in which they live and the "indigenous" claims by the local people. For

5. Safran, "Diasporas in Modern Societies," 83–84. Cf. Safran, "Jewish Diaspora in a
Comparative and Theoretical Perspective," 37.

6. Cohen, *Global Diasporas*, 23.

7. For instance, see Cohen, *Global Diaspora*, 21–24; Kumari, *Diasporic Consciousness in the Select Novels of Chitra Anarjee Divakaruni*, 52; Sideri, "Diaspora of the Term
Diaspora," 32–47; Butler, "Defining Diaspora, Refining a Discourse," 189–219.

8. Clifford, "Diasporas," 306.

9. Clifford, "Diasporas," 307.

10. Clifford, "Diasporas," 307.

11. Clifford, "Diasporas," 307.

throughout his essay, he understands the diaspora identity as a force that destabilizes both the nation-state and the claims of indigeneity.

Thus, Clifford argues that we need to think of this reality in terms of "diaspora consciousness."[12] This consciousness is marked by both positive and negative experiences. On the negative side, he argues that diaspora consciousness "is constituted negatively by experiences of discrimination and exclusion."[13] The experiences of discrimination and exclusion take place interconnectedly at racial, economic, and social levels. Particularly in the United States, diaspora communities are often racialized and exploited economically to meet the economic demand for productivity. On the positive side, he argues that "[d]iaspora consciousness is produced positively through identification with world-historical cultural/political forces, such as 'Africa' or 'China.'"[14] If the negative consciousness is constituted by the experience of exclusion, the positive consciousness is rooted in the longing to embrace, to be accepted. Because of that, diaspora identity often gives rise to a sense of globality, and universality—simply because the diaspora experience is a nomadic, transnational movement. "It is about feeling global," Clifford argues.[15]

I find Clifford's way of understanding the diaspora experience helpful because it does not automatically give the diaspora a positive spin. That way, each diaspora experience can be analyzed on the basis of its relationship with the others. Every diaspora community has its own unique dynamic with its others. Moreover, thinking of diaspora as consciousness can help us to interpret ancient *texts* that exist in front of us modern readers in the form of words. Because language functions to represent not only one's thoughts but also one's experiences, Paul's letters can point to us a diaspora consciousness.

In the following, I focus on Paul's statement in Rom 3 and its immediate literary context in Romans. This is not a comprehensive examination of

12. Clifford, "Diasporas," 311. Steven Vertovec calls this way of defining diaspora a "type of consciousness." He argues that there are three ways of defining diaspora: 1) diaspora as a social form, 2) diaspora as a type of consciousness, and 3) diaspora as a mode of cultural production. Clifford's definition falls under the second category. See Steven Vertovec, "Three Meanings of 'Diaspora,'" 277–99.

13. Clifford, "Diasporas," 311.

14. Clifford, "Diasporas," 312.

15. Clifford, "Diasporas," 312.

Pauline theology from a diaspora lens, but it is, I hope, a useful beginning in an area of Pauline studies that needs a lot more work.[16]

A Diaspora Reading of Rom 3:21–26

Paul is a diaspora Jew. The book of Acts records that he was born in Tarsus of Cilicia (Acts 22:3). How his family moved to Tarsus is open to a lot of speculation. Scholars have debated the next clause in Acts 22:3 that he was brought up in "this city." To which city was he referring? Jerusalem or Tarsus? Willem Cornelis van Unnik and Martin Hengel have challenged the idea that Paul was raised in Tarsus.[17] He might have been born in Tarsus, they say, but he spent most of his childhood in Jerusalem. Although this debate is important, it is not something that erases Paul's experience as a diaspora Jew. For even if he grew up in Jerusalem and spent his childhood there, we know from his letters that he spent a lot of time outside Jerusalem. Paul lived a diaspora life. Jerome Murphy-O'Connor, quoting Paul's statement in Rom 11:1 that he is "an Israelite, a descendant of Abraham, a member of the tribe of Benjamin," argues that such a statement that "affirm[s] his Jewish credentials betrays the expatriate, i.e., a Jew living in the Diaspora."[18] For, "[o]nly the descendants of those who emigrated from Ireland to the United States find it necessary to insist that they are Irish."[19] In short, Paul's insistence that he is a Hebrew born of Hebrews (Phil 3:3) is an indicator of his diaspora status.

With regards to Paul's statement in Rom 3, Robert Jewett attempts to break out of the trend of theological correctness in understanding these verses by bringing some social analysis to the interpretation of these famous verses.[20] Commenting on 3:22 in which Paul speaks of the righteous-

---

16. The analysis of Paul's theology from a diaspora point of view can be found in the following works: Charles, *Paul and the Politics of Diaspora*; Barclay, "Paul Among Diaspora Jews," 89–119; Barclay, *Pauline Churches and Diaspora Jews*; Wan, "Does Diaspora Identity Imply Some Sort of Universality?," 107–33; Wan, "Betwixt and Between," 137–229.

17. Hengel, *Pre-Christian Paul*.

18. Murphy-O'Connor, *Paul*, 32.

19. Murphy-O'Connor, *Paul*, 32.

20. Jewett complains that the discussion on *pistis* among New Testament scholars, particularly those who argue that πίστις Χριστοῦ is a subjective genitive (i.e., the faithfulness *of* Christ), has been focused mainly on "an intellectualized and dogmatized conception of faith, but it tends to lose sight of the social dimension of the very early usage in

ness of God through faith in (Jewett thinks that this is an objective genitive) Christ, Jewett states that, "In Christ divine righteousness acts to counter the arrogance of the dominant groups and the shame of the subordinate."[21] This is an interesting hermeneutical move to examine Paul's theology in an honor-shame framework. For Jewett, the righteousness (*dikaiosune*) of God in verse 24 is about "the restoration of honor."[22] He explains further that the verb δικαιούμενοι has to be understood as "being set right" or "declared upright" in a sense that "in Christ they [believers] are given honorable relationship."[23] The work of Christ, therefore, is to transfer one's shame into honor. For, "[in] being honored by God through Christ who died for all, the formerly shamed are integrated into the community of the saints in which this transformation process occurs, under the lordship of Christ."[24] In other words, Paul demonstrates that through "Christ's shameful death" God brings humanity into an "honorable relationship that results in . . . an actual transformation derived from the mirror image of Christ."[25]

Jewett's interpretative move comes from what is called the "socio-scientific approach" to the Bible.[26] Some biblical scholars draw on the works of anthropologists of the Mediterranean society (i.e., Mediterraneanism), particularly the works of modern anthropologists in the 1960s. The works of British anthropologists such as David Gilmore, Julian Pitt-Rivers, and John G. Peristiany were particularly influential in establishing this trend in the anthropological studies of Mediterranean societies.[27] Instead of a detailed analysis of honor and shame, how it has been employed in reading

---

which πίστις/πιστεύω functioned in as broadly defined jargon for participation in the community of the converted." See Jewett, *Romans*, 277.

21. See Jewett, *Romans*, 275.

22. See Jewett, *Romans*, 281.

23. See Jewett, *Romans*, 281.

24. See Jewett, *Romans*, 281.

25. See Jewett, *Romans*, 280–82.

26. There is a large body of literature in biblical studies on honor and shame. What follows is only a sampling. See Malina, "Social Sciences and Biblical Interpretation Reflections on Tradition and Practice," 229–42; Malina, *Social-Science Commentary on the Letters of Paul*; Malina, *New Testament World*; Pilch, *Social Scientific Models for Interpreting the Bible*; deSilva, *Honor, Patronage, Kinship, and Purity*; Rohrbaugh, "Honor," 109–25; Crook, "Honor, Shame, and Social Status Revisited," 591–611; Georges, "From Shame to Honor," 295–307; Neyrey, *Honor and Shame in the Gospel of Matthew*; Wu, *Reading Romans with Eastern Eyes*.

27. Peristiany, *Honour and Shame*; Gilmore, *Honor and Shame and the Unity of the Mediterranean*.

biblical texts, and its problems, here I note only two things. First, this Mediterraneanist project—mainly by British anthropologists—suffers from an orientalist problem. Paul Michael Johnson notes, for example, that:

> honor and shame have often been entangled in the kinds of stereotypical or unquestioned essentialisms that sought to relegate Mediterranean cultures to a more irrational and uncivilized status than that of their northern European counterparts, a phenomenon not unrelated to the imperial and ideological interests behind the Black Legend (which was partly fuelled by Spain's association with the Inquisition).[28]

Similarly, Edward Said notes that orientalists such as Harold Glidden in 1970 have used honor and shame to depict the Arabs (and Islam in general) as the people who see revenge as a virtue.[29] It is consequently no surprise that recent anthropologists have largely abandoned the inquiry into the Mediterranean society through an honor-shame framework.[30] Second, the honor and shame framework is a reductionist approach, for it reduces the complexity of Mediterranean societies to two essentialist cores of their culture. The word "honor" in English, for instance, cannot represent the richness of its parallel words in Greek, Egyptian, Italian, etc.[31] They are all flattened into an English word "honor." A similar reductionistic approach also can be seen in Jewett's insistence that the words "'righteousness,' 'honor,' and 'glory,'" in Rom 3 "can be used as virtually synonymous terms."[32] What is going on here is quite simple: Jewett employs a bigger category of "honor" to read Romans, and then he reduces all the words that are similar to it as pointing to honor. Such a reductionist move is both necessary and unavoidable. All this is to say that reading Paul's argument through an honor-shame lens is problematic at the cultural and political levels for it represents exclusively the gaze of white men.

Shifting our gaze, I propose that reading this text from a diaspora consciousness might provide a better alternative. Through a diaspora lens, Paul's passionate argument in Rom 3:21–26 demonstrates his move from

28. Johnson, "'Salido a La Vergüenza,'" 343.

29. Said, *Orientalism*, 48.

30. See more detailed discussions on this trend in Engelke, *How to Think Like an Anthropologist*; Albera, "Anthropology of the Mediterranean," 109–33; Herzfeld, "Honour and Shame," 339–51.

31. Wikan, "Shame and Honour," 635–52.

32. Jewett, "Honor and Shame in the Argument of Romans," 270.

alienation to inclusion. Paul made this argument because of his social location: he is a person with a diaspora consciousness. First of all, the experience of alienation, discrimination, and exclusion creates a negative consciousness which is apparent in Paul's discourse on sin. And here a brief exploration of Paul's argument leading to Rom 3:21–26 is necessary.

After expressing his thanksgiving and that he always remembers in his prayers (1:8–10) those whom he calls "God's beloved in Rome" (1:7) in his prayers (1:8–10), Paul tells them that he really wants to visit them in Rome (1:13). Paul seems to use this letter as a way of introducing himself to these people in Rome before he physically goes there. In 1:14–15, he tells them that "I am a debtor both to *Greeks and to barbarians*, both to the wise and the foolish—hence my eagerness to proclaim the gospel to you also who are in Rome." How does his eagerness to evangelize those who live in Rome have anything to do with the Greeks and barbarians? Why does not he just say, "I am a debtor to the Romans?" I suggest the reason has something to do with Paul's immediate experience as a diaspora Jew who lives among the Greeks. It reflects Paul's perspective rather than that of a person living in Rome. As someone who has not been to Rome, someone who has in fact lived most of his life in the eastern Mediterranean, Paul can only imagine his ethnic others as Greeks. It is his experience with the Greeks that gives him insights into the people of Rome. Here, Robin Cohen helpfully points out that "an identification with a diaspora serves to bridge the gap between the local and the global."[33] Similarly, in his analysis of the African diaspora in the Caribbean islands, Stuart Hall argues that the diaspora life is marked by three "presences": "*Presence Africaine, Presence Européenne, and Presence Americain.*"[34] Every African diaspora person in the Caribbean has experienced the dynamic interconnectedness of these three presences. Paul, in this context, is faced with three presences: Jewishness, Greekness, and Romanness.

The gentiles in Paul's diasporic imagination have a quite specific and narrow signification: they are *the Greeks and the barbarians*.[35] Why? Because living among those who speak Greek would limit his imagination. Thus, Caroline Johnson Hodge is right to observe that the word *gentiles* is never paired with *Jews* in Pauline letters, only the word *Greeks*. Drawing on the insights of Stanley Stowers, she points out that the signifier *Greeks* has

33. Cohen, *Global Diasporas*, 516.
34. Hall, "Cultural Identity and Diaspora," 230.
35. Wan, *Romans*, 24.

a connotation of social and political domination. "The term 'Greek,' when paired with 'Ioudaios,' could represent any non-Jewish people who live under Greek influence, which would include much of the world known to Paul," she explains.[36] If Paul had lived in Egypt, maybe he would have said, "I am a debtor to the Egyptians." But because he lives among the Greeks, he sees them and their others as his immediate ethnic others. In his fascinating study on the ethnic conflict in the Greco-Roman world, Christopher D. Stanley argues that Josephus uses the phrase *the Greeks* to signify "the primary oppressors of the Jews in Asia Minor."[37]

As a diaspora person, Paul understandably finds himself in between Greekness and Jewishness, i.e., between his ethnic origin and his ethnic other. It is no surprise that the expression "to the Jews first and also to the Greek" appears three times in Romans (1:16; 2:9,10). Paul's rhetorical description of the gentiles (i.e., the Greeks) in 1:18–32 reflects his strangeness from them more than it does the reality itself. In other words, painting them as ungodly and wicked, living only by passion and lust, shameless, etc., is a reflection of Paul's sense of difference, his sense of alienation, as a diaspora person. Not only does Paul describe the gentiles as the others, but he turns to those who call themselves "Jews" and speaks about them who boast about the law and circumcision. Here I follow Matthew Thiessen's suggestion that Paul's main interlocutors in 2:17–29 are gentiles. [38] These are the people who are gentiles but follow Jewish practices such as circumcision. They are proselytes. Paul still finds them strange—in spite of the fact that they claim to be Jewish. I felt the same way a few years ago when a missionary came to visit the Indonesian diaspora community in Los Angeles. He spoke the Indonesian language, wore batik, and ate Indonesian foods with us. Although he presented himself as an Indonesian, he was nonetheless a stranger to me. Here Paul likewise expresses how odd it is for a circumcised Greek to boast of their relationship with God, to think that they are a corrector of others, a teacher, and so on (2:17–24). For Paul, circumcision without obeying the law becomes quite meaningless. "Circumcision indeed is of value if you obey the law, but if you break the law, your circumcision has become uncircumcision,"

36. Johnson Hodge, *If Sons*, 59.

37. Stanley, "'Neither Jew Nor Greek,'" 107.

38. See Thiessen, "Paul's Argument against Gentile Circumcision in Romans 2:17–29," 373–91.

he states in 2:25. The idea of obeying the law he subsequently connects to the circumcision of the heart (2:28–29).

The next part of his argument is predictable. Paul addresses Jewishness and asks: What is the advantage of being a Jew (3:1–8)? What is the value of circumcision? He answers that the special place of Jewishness has to do with being entrusted with the oracles of God (3:2). He does not stop there. He also adds that some Jews are unfaithful. This unfaithfulness (ἀπιστία), however, will not nullify God's unfaithfulness (τὴν πίστιν τοῦ θεοῦ), Paul argues in 3:3–4. How do we understand unfaithfulness (ἀπιστία) here? Such a negative statement can be read as Paul's uneasiness with those who, for whatever reason or in whatever way, are unfaithful or compromise their Jewish identity. This is Paul's struggle with what it means to be Jewish, which in his view, some have not lived up to.

With that in mind, in Rom 3:4 he then casts an even bigger net by saying that "everyone is a liar" (πᾶς δὲ ἄνθρωπος ψεύστης). People who read Paul will discover that he is a master of exaggeration. He loves using over-the-top statements. Krister Stendahl once called this behavior annoying.[39] Does this mean that everyone is *in fact* a liar? Is really he stating a fact? Or is he expressing an internal struggle as a diaspora person who is feeling alienated from both the Greek world and the Jewish world? If we assume the former, then the conclusion of the total depravity of humanity is almost inevitable. People who take Paul's word literally without considering its rhetorical aim would reach the blanket conclusion that everyone—every person in the world—is a liar. If we assume the latter, then Paul's statement does not reflect reality but Paul's *perception* of reality. That is to say, casting everyone as a liar is more a demonstration of Paul's internal struggle as a diaspora person than an accurate description of everyone's reality. It reflects his struggle with the feeling of alienation, strangeness, or separation. Paul seems to feel that everyone is lying to him and that only God is true. This negative consciousness, as Clifford describes above, is a common experience among diaspora people.

Now, if we read further in Rom 3, the word πᾶς (everyone/all) actually has a specific point of reference. Paul states: "What then? Are we any better off? No, not at all; for we have already charged that all, both Jews and Greeks (Ἰουδαίους τε καὶ Ἕλληνας πάντας), are under the power of sin (ἁμαρτία)" (3:9). The πᾶς specifically refers to Jews and Greeks. Paul is not pointing to everyone in a generic sense. The "everyone" has ethnic specificity. In

---

39. Stendahl, *Paul among Jews and Gentiles and Other Essays*, 100.

addition to this, another thing we should note about Paul's view of the Jews and the Greeks is that he always gives Jewishness priority. The expression "to the Jews first and also to the Greek" to which I have alluded above points to the fact that he still understands this ethnic dynamic from a Jewish point of view. According to Hodge, this expression shows that "Paul maintains a hierarchy between the two, placing Jews at the top."[40] Or as Mark Nanos notes, "[Paul's] argument is still for 'the Jew first and also the Greek'; his intention is to bring about the certain restoration of all Israel and also the inclusion of the nations."[41] Stephen Young similarly argues that Paul's thought here is constructed around the gentiles receiving blessings through a Judean god.[42] That is to say, Paul still filters his understanding of the ethnic dynamic in the diaspora through a Jewish perspective.

This leads us to the universal statements that Paul makes in 3:21–26. There are two sides to Paul's statement here: the negative and the positive. Negatively, Paul argues that all have sinned (πάντες . . . ἥμαρτον). If we read "all" here as referring specifically to Jews and Greeks, then Paul is not wrestling with an ontological state of human being, but rather with how to make sense of his lived reality as a person who lives in between, in the liminality of Jewishness *and* Greekness. This is a state that is often very disorienting for people who are in the diaspora. His sense of exclusion, or what Clifford calls negative consciousness, he expresses quite strongly by casting them all as having failed (ἥμαρτον) and fallen short of the glory of God (3:23). This negative theology derives from a common diaspora experience of exclusion and alienation.

Positively, on the other side, although everyone has sinned, Paul continues by arguing that the key to solving this problem is πίστις (trust, faith, faithfulness). It seems as if Paul thinks that the only way to overcome alienation, sin, the exclusion, is to build trust and faithfulness. But this trust has to be grounded somewhere. That ground, for Paul, can be found in Jesus Christ. In 2:22, he states that it is through the faithfulness of Jesus Christ (διὰ πίστεως Ἰησοῦ Χριστοῦ), that the righteousness/justice of God (δικαιοσύνη θεοῦ) has been revealed for all (πάντας) who believe. Moving away from the sense of alienation, Paul thinks that through the faithfulness of Jesus Christ everyone is now included in the justice of God. In other

40. Johnson Hodge, *If Sons,* 138.

41. Nanos, "Jewish Context of the Gentile Audience Addressed in Paul's Letter to the Romans," 291.

42. Young, "Paul's Ethnic Discourse on 'Faith,'" 30–51.

words, it is through the work and life of Jesus Christ that everyone is included. Paul then elaborates on the details of the procedure by which the works of Christ in 3:24–26 are effective in everyone.

Now he quite emphatically adds, "For there is no distinction." Here he specifically refers to the Jews and the Greeks that I have discussed above. But how do we understand this statement? Is he dissolving the ethnic differences by erasing people's uniqueness and identity? Sze-kar Wan's insights into studying Paul's dealing with the Galatians might be helpful here. For Wan, what Paul is trying to do is to reconfigure the Galatians' new identity through a Jewish covenant "not by erasing ethnic and cultural differences but by *combining these differences into a hybrid existence*."[43] This is a Pauline "version of universalism."[44] I think Wan's diaspora analysis of Galatians is relevant also to Romans and our particular text. The positive aspect of the diaspora consciousness is marked by a sense of universality, a global feeling—as I have discussed above. It is because people in the diaspora want to be accepted, to be included. So what we see here in Rom 3 is an argument for a move from alienation to inclusion, from negative to positive consciousness.

Conclusion

Recall my opening statement about my student who cannot understand white European discourses on the New Testament because she does not see herself reflected in the reading because it is not her story. To move away from a European story that is often treated as a universal story, a standard story requires an act of exploration of different social experiences. This is precisely what I have attempted to do in this chapter.

Paul's negative picture of humanity in Rom 3 is not actually a reflection of humanity itself, but a reflection of his diaspora experience of alienation and exclusion. His christological argument that through the faithfulness of Christ, the justice of God to humanity is revealed, also reflects his diasporic desire to be included and to be accepted. Although life in the diaspora is often hard, Paul finds the solution to his diasporic struggle in God through the faithfulness of Christ. Such solutions are hopeful. No wonder Avtar Brah describes life in the diaspora as follows:

43. Italics are his. Wan, "Does Diaspora Identity Imply Some Sort of Universality?," 126.

44. Wan, "Does Diaspora Identity Imply Some Sort of Universality?," 127.

The word diaspora often invokes the imagery of traumas of separation and dislocation, and this is certainly a very important aspect of the migratory experience. But diasporas are also potentially the sites of hope and new beginnings. They are contested cultural and political terrains where individual and collective memories collide, reassemble and reconfigure.[45]

Indeed, Rom 3 reflects Paul's reconfiguration of his diaspora imagination, his attempt to make sense of his traumas of separation, exclusion, and dislocation.

45. Brah, *Cartographies of Diaspora*, 190.

Bibliography

Aasgaard, Reidar. "'Brotherly Advice': Christian Siblingship and New Testament Paraenesis." In *Early Christian Paraenesis in Context*, edited by James M. Starr and Troels Engberg-Pedersen, 237–66. New York: Walter De Gruyter, 2004.

Agosto, Efrain. "Islands, Borders, and Migration: Reading Paul in Light of the Crisis in Puerto Rico." In *Latinxs, the Bible and Migration*, edited by Efrain Agosto and Jacqueline M. Hidalgo, 149–70. Cham, Switzerland: Palgrave Macmillan, 2018.

Agyare, Giselle. "My Race Is a Part of my Identity but My Christian Faith Comes First." Https://faithbeliefforum.org/my-race-is-part-of-my-identity-but-my-christian-faith-comes-first/.

Albera, Dionigi. "Anthropology of the Mediterranean: Between Crisis and Renewal." *History and Anthropology* 17 (2006) 109–33.

Albizu-Campos Meneses, Laura, and Mario A. Rodríguez León. *Albizu Campos: Escritos.* Hato Rey, PR: Publicaciones Puertorriqueñas, 2007.

Albizu Campos, Pedro. "La retirada americana de Santo Domingo." In *El Nacionalista de Ponce*, Puerto Rico, July 13, 1925. Reproduced in Laura Albizu-Campos Meneses & Mario A. Rodríguez León, *Albizu Campos: Escritos*. Hato Rey, PR: Publicaciones Puertorriqueñas, 2007.

———. "Notas sobre el caso de Puerto Rico." In Laura Albizu-Campos Meneses & Mario A. Rodríguez León, *Albizu Campos: Escritos*. Hato Rey, PR: Publicaciones Puertorriqueñas, 2007.

Ashcroft, Bill, et al. *The Empire Writes Back: Theory and Practice in Postcolonial Literatures.* London: Routledge, 1989.

Aune, David E. *The Westminster Dictionary of New Testament and Early Christian Literature and Rhetoric.* Louisville, KY: Westminster John Knox, 2003.

Ayala Santiago, Mario O. *Orden y Palabra en Los Discursos de Pedro Albizu Campos.* Rio Piedras, PR: Publicaciones Gaviota, 2008.

Bakirtzis, Charalambos, and Helmut Koester, eds. *Philippi at the Time of Paul and After His Death.* Harrisburg, PA: Trinity, 1998.

Barclay, John M. G. "Paul Among Diaspora Jews: Anomaly or Apostate?" *Journal for the Study of the New Testament* 18 (1996) 89–119.

———. *Pauline Churches and Diaspora Jews.* Grand Rapids: Eerdmans, 2016.

Barrett, C. K. *The Epistle to the Romans.* Grand Rapids: Baker, 2011.

Bartlett, David Lyon. *Romans.* Louisville, KY: Westminster John Knox, 1995.

Betz, Hans D. *Galatians: A Commentary on Paul's Letter to the Churches in Galatia.* Hermeneia. Philadelphia: Fortress, 1979.

Bhabha, Homi K. *The Location of Culture.* London: Routledge, 2004.

Blackburn, Robin. *The Making of New World Slavery: From the Baroque to the Modern, 1492–1700.* London: Verso, 2010.

Bowens, Lisa M. *African American Readings of Paul: Reception, Resistance & Transformation.* Grand Rapids: Eerdmans, 2020.

Boyarin, Daniel. *A Radical Jew: Paul and the Politics of Identity.* Berkeley: University of California, 1994.

Brah, Avtar. *Cartographies of Diaspora: Contesting Identities.* London: Routledge, 1996.

Braxton, Brad R. *No Longer Slaves: Galatians and African American Experience.* Collegeville, MN: Liturgical, 2002.

Brecht Martin. *Martin Luther Volume Three: The Preservation of the Church 1532–1546.* Translated by J. L. Schaaf. Minneapolis: Fortress, 1993.

Bruce, F. F. *The Epistle to the Galatians: A Commentary on the Greek Text.* Grand Rapids: Eerdmans, 1982.

Buell, Denise K. "Rethinking the Relevance of Race for early Christian Self-Definition." *Harvard Theological Review* 94 (2001) 449–76.

———. *Why This New Race? Ethnic Reasoning in Early Christianity.* New York: Columbia University Press, 2005.

Buell, Denise K., and Caroline Johnson Hodge. "The Politics of Interpretation: The Rhetoric of Race and Ethnicity in Paul." *Journal of Biblical Literature* 123 (2004) 235–51.

Burton, Ernest DeWitt. *A Critical and Exegetical Commentary on the Epistle to the Galatians.* Edinburgh: T. & T. Clark, 1921.

Butler, Kim D. "Defining Diaspora, Refining a Discourse." *Diaspora: A Journal of Transnational Studies* 10 (2001) 189–219.

Byrne, Brendan *Romans.* Collegeville, MN: Liturgical, 1996.

Carroll, David. "In Memoriam: Jacques Derrida, Professor of English and Comparative Literature, French and Italian, and Philosophy." University of California Academic Senate, 2004. https://senate.universityofcalifornia.edu/_files/inmemoriam/html/JacquesDerrida.htm.

Carson, D. A. "Atonement in Romans 3:21–26." In *The Glory of the Atonement: Biblical, Theological Practical Perspectives,* edited by Charles E. Hill and Frank A. James III, 119–39. Downers Grove, IL: InterVarsity, 2004.

Cassidy, Richard. *Paul in Chains: Roman Imprisonment and the Letters of St. Paul.* New York: Crossroad, 2001.

Castelli, Elizabeth. *Imitating Paul: A Discourse of Power.* Louisville, KY: Westminster John Knox, 1991.

Charles, Ronald. *Paul and the Politics of Diaspora.* Minneapolis: Fortress, 2014.

Cicero, *Against Verres.* Translated by L. H. G. Greenwood. *Cicero: The Verrine Orations, Volume I.* LCL 221. Cambridge, MA: Harvard University Press, 1928.

Clifford, James. "Diasporas." *Cultural Anthropology* 9 (1994) 302–38.

Cohen, Robin. *Global Diasporas: An Introduction.* 2nd ed. London: Routledge, 2008.

Cohen, Shaye. *The Beginnings of Jewishness.* Berkeley: University of California, 1999.

Collange, J.-F. *L'Epître de Saint Paul aux Philippiens.* Neuchâtel: Delachaux & Niestlé, 1973.

Copeland, M. Shawn. *Knowing Christ Crucified: The Witness of African American Religious Experience*. Maryknoll, NY: Orbis, 2018.

Crook, Zeba. "Honor, Shame, and Social Status Revisited." *Journal of Biblical Literature* 128 (2009) 591–611.

Das, A. Andrew. *Galatians*. Concordia Commentary. Saint Louis: Concordia, 2014.

Daniels, Jessie. *White Lies: Race, Class, Gender, and Sexuality in White Supremacist Discourse*. London: Routledge, 1997.

Denis, Nelson. *War Against All Puerto Ricans: Revolution and Terror in America's Colony* New York: Nation, 2015.

Derrida, Jacques. "Force of Law: The 'Mystical Foundation of Authority.'" In *Deconstruction and the Possibility of Justice*, edited by Drucilla Cornell et al., 3–67. London: Routledge, 1992.

———. *Of Hospitality: Anne Dufourmantelle Invites Jacques Derrida to Respond*. Translated by Rachel Bowlby. Stanford: Stanford University Press, 2000.

deSilva, David A. *Honor, Patronage, Kinship, and Purity: Unlocking New Testament Culture*. Downers Grove, IL: InterVarsity, 2022.

———. *The Letter to the Galatians*. Grand Rapids: Eerdmans, 2018.

Dickerson, Febbie C. "Acts 9:36–43: Many Faces of Tabitha, a Womanist Reading." In *I Found God in Me: A Womanist Biblical Hermeneutics Reader*, edited by Mitzi J. Smith, 296–312. Eugene, OR: Wipf & Stock, 2015.

Dunn, James D. G. *Romans 9–16*. Dallas: Word, 1988.

Earl, Riggins. *Dark Symbols, Obscure Signs: God, Self, and Community in the Slave Mind*. Knoxville, TN: University of Tennessee, 2003.

Easter, Matthew C. "The Pistis Christou Debate: Main Arguments and Responses in Summary." *Currents in Biblical Research* 9 (2010) 33–47.

Elliott, Neil. *The Arrogance of the Nations: Reading Romans in the Shadow of Empire*. Minneapolis: Fortress, 2008.

Engberg-Pederson, Troels. "The Concept of Paraenesis." In *Early Christian Paraenesis in Context*, edited by James M. Starr and Troels Engbert-Pederson, 47–72. New York: De Gruyter, 2004.

Engelke, Matthew. *How to Think Like an Anthropologist*. Princeton, NJ: Princeton University Press, 2019.

Esler, Philip F. *Conflict and Identity in Romans: The Social Setting of Paul's Letter*. Minneapolis: Fortress, 2003.

Fee, Gordon. *Paul's Letter to the Philippians*. Grand Rapids: Eerdmans, 1995.

Fredriksen, Paula. *Paul: The Pagans' Apostle*. New Haven, CT: Yale University Press, 2017.

Furnish, Victor P. *Theology and Ethics in Paul*. Nashville: Abingdon, 1968.

Georges, Jayson. "From Shame to Honor: A Theological Reading of Romans for Honor-Shame Contexts." *Missiology* 38 (2010) 295–307.

Gerbner, Katharine. *Christian Slavery: Conversion and Race in the Protestant Atlantic World*. Philadelphia: University of Pennsylvania Press, 2018.

Gilmore, David G., ed. *Honor and Shame and the Unity of the Mediterranean*. Washington, D.C: American Anthropological Association, 1987.

Glancy, Jennifer A. *Slavery in Early Christianity*. Oxford: Oxford University Press, 2002.

Gnilka, Joachim. *Der Philipperbrief*. Freiburg: Herder, 1976.

Gonzalez, Juan. *Harvest of Empire: A History of Latinos in America*. New York: Penguin, 2000.

Goode, Richard. "The Death of the Apostle Paul." https://bibleresearchtoday.com/2019/02/27/the-death-of-the-apostle-paul/.

Hall, Stuart. "Cultural Identity and Diaspora." In *Identity: Community, Culture, Difference*, edited by Jonathan Rutherford, 222–37. London: Lawrence & Wishart, 1990.

Hays, Richard B. "Psalm 143 and the Logic of Romans 3." *Journal of Biblical Literature* 99 (1980) 107–15.

Hengel, Martin. *The Pre-Christian Paul*. London: SCM, 1991.

Henson, Josiah. *An Autobiography of the Rev. Josiah Henson ("Uncle Tom"). From 1789 to 1881*. London, Ontario: Schuyler, Smith & Co., 1881.

———. *Father Henson's Story of His Own Life*. Boston: John P. Jewett, 1858.

———. *The Life of Josiah Henson, Formerly a Slave, Now an Inhabitant of Canada, as Narrated by Himself*. Boston: Arthur D. Phelps, 1849.

———. *Truth Stranger than Fiction: Father Henson's Story of His Own Life*. Boston: John P. Jewett, 1858.

Herzfeld, Michael. "Honour and Shame: Problems in the Comparative Analysis of Moral Systems." *Man* 15 (1980) 339–51.

Horrell, David. "Paul, Inclusion and Whiteness: Particularizing Interpretation." *Journal for the Study of the New Testament* 40 (2017) 123–47.

Horsley, Richard A. *1 Corinthians*. Abingdon New Testament Commentaries. Nashville: Abingdon, 1998.

———, ed. *Paul and Empire: Religion and Power in Roman Imperial Society* Valley Forge, PA: Trinity, 1997.

Hultgren, Arland J. *Paul's Letter to the Romans: A Commentary*. Grand Rapids: Eerdmans, 2011.

Hussey, Ian. "A Theology of Church Engagement: A Reflection on the Practice of the Early Churches." *Colloquium* 44 (2012) 208–25.

Hutchison, William. *Errand to the World: American Protestant Thought and Foreign Missions*. Chicago: The University of Chicago Press, 1987.

Jeremias, Joachim. "Einige vorwiegend sprachliche Beobachtungen zur Römer 11,25–36." In *Die Israelfrage nach Röm 9–11*, edited by L. de Lorenzi, 193–203. Biblical-Ecumenical Section 3. Rome: Abtei von St. Paul vor den Mauern, 1977.

Jewett, Robert. "Honor and Shame in the Argument of Romans." In *Putting Body and Soul Together: Essays in Honor of Robin Scroggs*, edited by Virginia Wiles et al., 258–73. Valley Forge, PA: Trinity, 1997.

———. *Romans: A Commentary*. Hermeneia: A Critical and Historical Commentary of the Bible. Minneapolis: Fortress, 2007.

Johnson Hodge, Caroline. *If Sons, Then Heirs: A Study of Kinship and Ethnicity in the Letters of Paul*. New York: Oxford University Press, 2007.

———. "The Question of Identity: gentiles and gentiles—but also Not—in Pauline Communities." In *Paul within Judaism: Restoring the First-Century Context to the Apostle*, edited by M. Nanos and M. Zetterholm, 153–73. Minneapolis: Fortress, 2015.

Jipp, Joshua W. *Saved by Faith and Hospitality*. Grand Rapids: Eerdmans, 2017.

Johnson, Luke Timothy. *Reading Romans: A Literary and Theological Commentary*. New York: Crossroad, 1997.

———. "Rom 3:21–26 and the Faith of Jesus." *The Catholic Biblical Quarterly* 44 (1982) 77–90.

Johnson, Paul Michael. "'Salido a La Vergüenza': Inquisition, Penality, and a Cervantine View of Mediterranean 'Values.'" *EHumanista/Cervantes* 2 (2013) 340–61.

Jordan, Winthrop D. *White Over Black; American Attitudes Toward the Negro, 1550–1812.* Baltimore, MD: Penguin, 1969.

Junta Pedro Albizu Campos. *Nervio y pulso del mundo: Nuevos Ensayos sobre Pedro Albizu Campos y el nacionalismo revolucionario.* San Juan, PR: Talla de Sombra Editores, 2014.

Kahl, Brigitte. "No Longer Male: Masculinity Struggles behind Galatians 3.28?" *Journal for Study of the New Testament* 79 (2000) 37–49.

Käsemann, Ernst. *Commentary on Romans.* Grand Rapids: Eerdmans, 1980.

———. "A Critical Analysis of Philippians 2.5–11." *Journal for Theology and Church* 5 (1968) 45–88.

Kearney, Richard. "Hospitality: Possible or Impossible?" *Hospitality and Society* 5 (2015) 173–84.

Keener, Craig. *Galatians: A Commentary.* Grand Rapids: Baker, 2019.

Kendi, Ibram X. *Stamped from the Beginning: The Definitive History of Racist Ideas in America.* New York: Nation, 2016.

Kim, Yung Suk. *Biblical Interpretation: Theory, Process, and Criteria.* Eugene, OR: Pickwick, 2013.

———. *Christ's Body in Corinth: The Politics of a Metaphor* (Paul in Critical Contexts). Minneapolis: Fortress, 2008.

———. *How to Read Paul: A Brief Introduction to His Theology, Writings, and World.* Minneapolis: Fortress, 2021.

———. ""Imitators" (Mimetai) in 1 Cor. 4:16 and 11:1: A New Reading of Threefold Embodiment." *Horizons in Biblical Theology* 33 (2011) 147–170.

———. *Messiah in Weakness: A Portrait of Jesus from the Perspective of the Dispossessed.* Eugene, OR: Cascade, 2016.

———. "Reclaiming Christ's Body (soma christou): Embodiment of God's Gospel in Paul's Letters." *Interpretation* 67 (2013) 20–29.

———. "Reevaluating Western Mission and Mission Texts: In the case of Korea in the Nineteenth Century." Unpublished paper.

———. *Reimagining the Body of Christ in Paul's Letters: In View of Paul's Gospel.* Eugene, OR: Resource, 2019.

———. *Rereading Galatians from the Perspective of Paul's Gospel: A Literary and Theological Commentary.* Eugene, OR: Cascade, 2019.

———. *Rereading Romans from the Perspective of Paul's Gospel: A Literary and Theological Commentary.* Eugene, OR: Resource, 2019.

———. *A Theological Introduction to Paul's Letters: Exploring a Threefold Theology of Paul.* Eugene, OR: Cascade, 2011.

Kittredge, Cynthia. *Community and Authority: The Rhetoric of Obedience in the Pauline Tradition.* Harrisburg, PA: Trinity, 1998.

Koenig, John. *New Testament Hospitality.* Philadelphia: Fortress, 1985.

Koester, Helmut. *Introduction to the New Testament. Volume 2: History and Literature of Early Christianity.* New York: Walter De Gruyter, 1995.

Kumari, P. Prasanna. *Diasporic Consciousness in the Select Novels of Chitra Anarjee Divakaruni.* Raleigh, NC: Lulu, 2018.

Lee, Michelle. *Paul, the Stoics, and the Body of Christ.* Cambridge: Cambridge University Press, 2006.

Longenecker, Richard. *Galatians*. Word. Dallas: Word, 1990.

Luther, Martin. *A Commentary on St. Paul's Epistle to the Galatians*. Philadelphia: Quaker City, 1875.

———. "The Jews and Their Lies." https://www.jewishvirtuallibrary.org/martin-luther-quot-the-jews-and-their-lies-quot.

MacDonald, Dennis R. *There is No Male and Female: The Fate of a Dominical Saying in Paul and Gnosticism*. Philadelphia: Fortress, 1987.

Malherbe, Abraham J. *Moral Exhortation: A Greco-Roman Sourcebook*. Philadelphia: Westminster, 1986.

Malina, Bruce J. *The New Testament World: Insights from Cultural Anthropology*. Louisville, KY: Westminster John Knox, 2001.

———. *Social-Science Commentary on the Letters of Paul*. Minneapolis: Augsburg, 2006.

———. "The Social Sciences and Biblical Interpretation Reflections on Tradition and Practice." *Interpretation* 36 (1982) 229–42.

Marchal, Joseph. "Queer Approaches: Improper Relations with Pauline Letters." In *Studying Paul's Letters: Contemporary Perspectives and Methods,* edited by J. Marchal, 209–27. Minneapolis: Fortress, 2012.

Martin, Ralph P. *Carmen Christi (Philippians 2.5–11 in Recent Interpretations and in the Setting of Early Worship*. Grand Rapids: Eerdmans, 1983.

Martyn, J. Louis. *Galatians: A New Translation with Introduction and Commentary*. Garden City, NY: Doubleday, 1997.

Matera, Frank J. *Romans*. Grand Rapids: Baker, 2010.

Meade, William. *Pastoral Letter: Religious Instruction of Servants*. Richmond, VA: Ellyson Printers, 1853–54.

Meeks, Wayne. *The First Urban Christians: The Social World of the Apostle Paul*. New Haven, CT: Yale University Press, 1983.

———. "The Image of the Androgyne: Some Uses of a Symbol in Earliest Christianity." *History of Religions* 13 (1974) 165–208.

———. "The Man from Heaven in Paul's Letter to the Philippians." In *The Future of Early Christianity: Essays in Honor of Helmut Koester,* edited by B. A. Pearson, 329–36. Minneapolis: Fortress, 1991.

Merode, Marie de. "Une théologie primitive de la femme?" *Revue théologique de Louvain* 9 (1978) 176–89.

Mitchell, Margaret. *Paul and the Rhetoric of Reconciliation: An Exegetical Investigation of the Language and Composition of 1 Corinthians*. Louisville, KY: Westminster John Knox, 1991.

Moiser, Jeremy. "Rethinking Romans 12–15." *New Testament Study* 36 (1990) 571–82.

Moo, Douglas J. *The Epistle to the Romans*. Grand Rapids: Eerdmans, 1996.

Morales, Ed. *Fantasy Island: Colonialism, Exploitation, and the Betrayal of Puerto Rico* New York: Bold Type, 2019.

Moule, C. F. D. "Further Reflections on Philippians 2:5–11." In *Apostolic History and the Gospel. Biblical and Historical Essays Presented to F. F. Bruce on his 60th Birthday,* edited by W. W. Gasque and R. P. Martin, 265–76. Grand Rapids: Eerdmans, 1970.

Murphy-O'Connor, Jerome. *Paul: A Critical Life*. New York: Oxford University Press, 1998.

Nadella, Raj. "Embrace, Ambivalence, and Theoxenia: New Testament Perspectives on Hospitality to Strangers." In *Christianity and the Law of Migration,* edited by Silas W. Allard et al., 165–78. London: Routledge, 2022.

Nanos, Mark D. "The Jewish Context of the Gentile Audience Addressed in Paul's Letter to the Romans." *The Catholic Biblical Quarterly* 61 (1999) 283–304.

Nebreda, Sergio R. *Christ Identity: A Social Scientific Reading of Philippians 2:5–11.* Göttingen: Vandenhoeck and Ruprecht, 2011.

Neyrey, Jerome H. *Honor and Shame in the Gospel of Matthew.* Louisville, KY: Westminster John Knox, 1998.

Nicols, John. "Hospitality among the Romans." In *The Oxford Handbook of Social Relations in the Roman World,* edited by Michael Peachin, 422–37. New York: Oxford University Press, 2011.

NPR. "White Supremacist Ideas Have Historical Roots In U.S. Christianity." https://www.npr.org/2020/07/01/883115867/white-supremacist-ideas-have-historical-roots-in-u-s-christianity.

Oakes, Peter. *Galatians.* Paideia. Grand Rapids: Baker, 2015.

O'Brien, Peter T. *Commentary on Philippians.* New International Greek New Testament Commentary. Grand Rapids: Eerdmans, 1991.

Odell-Scott, David. "Let the Women Speak in Church: An Egalitarian Interpretation of First Corinthians 14:33b–36." *Biblical Theological Bulletin* 13 (1983) 90–93.

Oepke, Albrecht. "δύω, κτλ." *Theological Dictionary of the New Testament* 2 (1964) 318–21.

Olbricht, Thomas H., and Jeffrey L. Sumney, eds. *Paul and Pathos.* Atlanta: Society of Biblical Literature, 2001.

Origen. "Homily V." Trans. Ronald E. Heine. *Origen: Homilies on Genesis and Exodus.* Washington: Catholic University of America, 1982.

Perkins, Pheme. "Christology, Friendship and Finances in Philippians." SBL Seminar Papers 26, 509–20. Atlanta: Scholars, 1987.

———. "Philippians: Theology of the Heavenly Polituema." In *Pauline Theology,* edited by J. M. Bassler, 89–104. Minneapolis: Fortress, 1991.

Peristiany, John G. *Honour and Shame: The Values of Mediterranean Society.* Chicago: University of Chicago, 1969.

Peterlin, Davorin. *Paul's Letter to the Philippians in Light of Disunity in the Church.* New York: Brill, 1995.

Petersen, Norman. *Rediscovering Paul: Philemon and the Sociology of Paul's Narrative World.* Philadelphia: Fortress, 1985.

Peterson, Eugene. *Christ Plays in Ten Thousand Places.* Winnipeg: CMBC Publications, 1999.

Pilch, John J. *Social Scientific Models for Interpreting the Bible: Essays by the Context Group in Honor of Bruce J. Malina.* Leiden: Brill, 2001.

Piper, John. "Strategic Hospitality." Desiring God. August 25, 1985. https://www.desiringgod.org/messages/strategic-hospitality.

Pohl, Christine D. *Making Room: Recovering Hospitality as a Christian Tradition.* Grand Rapids: Eerdmans, 1999.

Popkes, Wiard. "Paraenesis in the New Testament. An Exercise in Conceptuality." In *Early Christian Paraenesis in Context,* edited by James Starr and Troels Engberg-Pedersen, 13–46. Boston: De Gruyter, 2012.

Raboteau, Albert J. *Slave Religion: The "Invisible Institution" in the Antebellum South.* Updated Edition. Oxford and New York: Oxford University Press, 1978.

Reese, Ruth Anne, and Steven Ybarrola. "Racial and Ethnic Identity: Social Scientific and Biblical Perspectives in Dialogue." *The Asbury Journal* 65 (2010) 65–82.

Reumann, John. "The Gospel of the Righteousness of God: Pauline Reinterpretation in Romans 3:21–31." *Interpretation* 20 (1966) 432–52.

Ribbens, Benjamin J. "Forensic-Retributive Justification in Romans 3:21–26: Paul's Doctrine of Justification in Dialogue with Hebrews." *The Catholic Biblical Quarterly* 74 (2012) 548–67.

Roetzel, Calvin J. *The Letters of Paul: Conversations in Context.* 5th ed. Louisville, KY: Westminster John Knox, 2009.

Rohrbaugh, Richard L. "Honor: Core Value in the Biblical World." In *Understanding the Social World of the New Testament*, edited by Dietmar Neufeld and Richard DeMaris, 109–25. London: Routledge, 2009.

Rosario Natal, Carmelo. *Albizu Campos: Preso en Atlanta. Historia del Reo #51298-A (Correspondencia).* San Juan, PR: Producciones Históricas, 2001.

Safran, William. "Diasporas in Modern Societies: Myths of Homeland and Return." *Diaspora: A Journal of Transnational Studies* 1 (1991) 83–99.

———. "The Jewish Diaspora in a Comparative and Theoretical Perspective." *Israel Studies* 10 (2005) 36–60.

Said, Edward W. *Orientalism.* New York: Penguin, 2003.

Sanders, E. P. *Paul, the Law, and the Jewish People.* Philadelphia: Fortress, 1983.

Schüssler Fiorenza, Elizabeth. "The Ethics of Biblical Interpretation: Decentering Biblical Scholarship." *Journal of Biblical Literature* 107 (1988) 3–17.

———. *The Power of the Word: Scripture and the Rhetoric of Empire.* Minneapolis: Fortress, 2007.

Sechrest, Love L. *A Former Jew: Paul and the Dialectics of Race.* London: T. & T. Clark International, 2009.

Segovia, Fernando F. "'And They Began to Speak in Other Tongues': Competing Modes of Discourse in Contemporary Biblical Criticism. In *Reading from This Place*, edited by Fernando F. Segovia and Mary Ann Tolbert, 1:1–32. Minneapolis: Fortress, 1995.

Seneca, *Controversiae.* Translated by Michael Winterbottom. *Seneca: Declamations, Volume II.* LCL 464. Cambridge, MA: Harvard University Press, 1974.

Sideri, Eleni. "The Diaspora of the Term Diaspora: A Working Paper of a Definition." *Transtext(e)s Transcultures* 跨文本跨文化. *Journal of Global Cultural Studies* 4 (2008) 32–47.

Smith, Mitzi J. "God's Righteousness, Christ's Faith/Fulness, and 'Justification by Faith Alone' (Romans 3:21–26)." In *Romans and the Legacy of St Paul: Historical, Theological, and Social Perspectives*, edited by P. G. Bolt and J. R. Harrison, 181–254. Macquarie Park: SCD, 2019.

Smith, Mitzi J., et al., eds. *Bitter the Chastening Rod: Africana Biblical Interpretation after Stoney the Road We Trod in the Age of BLM, SayHerName, and MeToo.* Minneapolis: Fortress, 2002.

Smither, Edward L. *Mission as Hospitality: Imitating the Hospitable God in Mission.* Eugene, OR: Cascade, 2021.

Songer, Harold S. "New Standing before God Romans 3:21–5:21." *Review and Expositor* 73 (1976) 415–24.

Stanley, Christopher D. "'Neither Jew Nor Greek': Ethnic Conflict in Graeco-Roman Society." *Journal for the Study of the New Testament* 19 (1997) 101–24.

Stendahl, Krister. *The Bible and the Role of Women: A Case in Hermeneutics.* Philadelphia: Fortress, 1966.

———. *Paul among Jews and Gentiles and Other Essays.* Philadelphia: Fortress, 1976.

Stevens-Arroyo, Anthony M. "The Catholic Worldview in the Political Philosophy of Pedro Albizu Campos: The Death Knoll of Puerto Rican Insularity." *U.S. Catholic Historian* 20 (2002) 53–73.

Thiessen, Matthew. "Paul's Argument against Gentile Circumcision in Romans 2:17–29." *Novum Testamentum* 56 (2014) 373–91.

Thiselton, Anthony C. *Discovering Romans: Content, Interpretation, Reception*. Grand Rapids: Eerdmans, 2016.

Thornwell, James Henley. "Relation to the Church on Slavery." In *The Collected Writings of James Henley Thornwell*, edited by John Adger and John Girardeau, 4:381–97. Richmond: Presbyterian Committee on Publications, 1873.

Tishby, Jemar. *The Color of Compromise: The Truth about the American Church's Complicity in Racism*. Grand Rapids: Zondervan Reflective, 2019.

Underwood, Horace G. *The Call of Korea: Political, Social, Religious*. New York: Young People's Missionary Movement of the United States and Canada, 1908.

Vertovec, Steven. "Three Meanings of 'Diaspora,' Exemplified among South Asian Religions." *Diaspora: A Journal of Transnational Studies* 6 (1997) 277–99.

Wan, Sze-kar. "Abraham and the Promise of Spirit: Points of Convergence between Philo and Paul." In *Things Revealed: Studies in Early Jewish and Christian Literature in Honor of Michael E. Stone*, edited by E. G. Chazon et al., 209–20. Leiden: Brill, 2004.

———. "Betwixt and Between: Toward Hermeneutics of Hyphenation." In *Ways of Being, Ways of Reading: Asian American Biblical Interpretation*, edited by Mary F. Foskett and Jeffrey Kah-Jin Kuan, 137–229. St. Louis, MO: Chalice, 2006.

———. "Does Diaspora Identity Imply Some Sort of Universality?" In *Interpreting Beyond Borders*, edited by Fernando F. Segovia, 107–33. Sheffield, UK: Sheffield, 2000.

———. "The Letter to the Galatians." In *A Postcolonial Commentary on the New Testament Writings*, edited by F. F. Segovia and R. S. Sugirtharajah, 246–64. London: T. & T. Clark, 2007.

———. "Mainstreaming the Minoritized." In *Paul's Gospel, Empire and Race and Ethnicity: Through the Lens of Minoritized Scholarship*, edited by Yung Suk Kim. Eugene, OR: Pickwick, 2023.

———. *Romans: An Introduction and Study Guide: Empire and Resistance*. T. & T. Clark Study Guides to the New Testament. London: T. & T. Clark, 2021.

———. "'To the Jew First and also to the Greek': Reading Romans as Ethnic Construction." In *Prejudice and Christian Beginnings: Investigating Race, Gender, and Ethnicity in Early Christianity*, edited by E. Schüssler Fiorenza and Laura Nasrallah, 129–55. Minneapolis: Augsburg/Fortress, 2009.

———. "Wrestling with 'Body of Christ' in an Age of Tribalism: Towards an Asian American Hermeneutics of Dissent." *Bible and Critical Theory* 16 (2020) 92–116.

Westmoreland, Mark W. "Interruptions: Derrida and Hospitality." *Kritike* 2 (2008) 1–10.

Wikan, Unni. "Shame and Honour: A Contestable Pair." *Man* 1 (1984) 635–52.

Williams, Demetrius K. *"Enemies of the Cross of Christ": The Terminology of the Cross and Conflict in Philippians*. London: Continuum, 2002.

———. "Philippians." In *Global Bible Commentary*, edited by Daniel Patte, 482–89. Nashville: Abingdon, 2004.

Wire, Antoinette Clark. *The Corinthian Women Prophets: A Reconstruction Through Paul's Rhetoric*. Minneapolis: Fortress, 1990.

Witherington, Ben, III. *Friendship and Finances in Philippi: The Letter of Paul to the Philippians*. Valley Forge, PA: Trinity, 1994.

————. "Rite and Rights for Women—Galatians 3.28." *New Testament Study* 27 (1981) 593–604.

Witherington, Ben, III, with Darlene Hyatt. *Paul's Letter to the Romans: A Socio-Rhetorical Commentary*. Grand Rapids: Eerdmans, 2004.

Wright, Jeremiah. "Who You Are in Christ Changes Everything about Race" (WayNation). https://waynation.com/wbsg/who-you-are-in-christ-changes-everything-racial-tension-the-bridge-church/.   https://www.youtube.com/watch?v=fNk1Vp-9DYg&t=745s.

Wright, N. T. *Galatians*. Grand Rapids: Eerdmans, 2021.

————. "Paul's Gospel and Caesar's Empire." In *Paul and Politics: Ecclesia, Israel, Imperium, Interpretation*, edited by Richard A. Horsley, 160–83. Harrisburg, PA: Trinity, 2000.

Wu, Jackson. *Reading Romans with Eastern Eyes: Honor and Shame in Paul's Message and Mission*. Downers Grove, IL: InterVarsity, 2019.

Young, Stephen L. "Paul's Ethnic Discourse on 'Faith': Christ's Faithfulness and Gentile Access to the Judean God in Romans 3:21—5:1." *Harvard Theological Review* 108 (2015) 30–51.